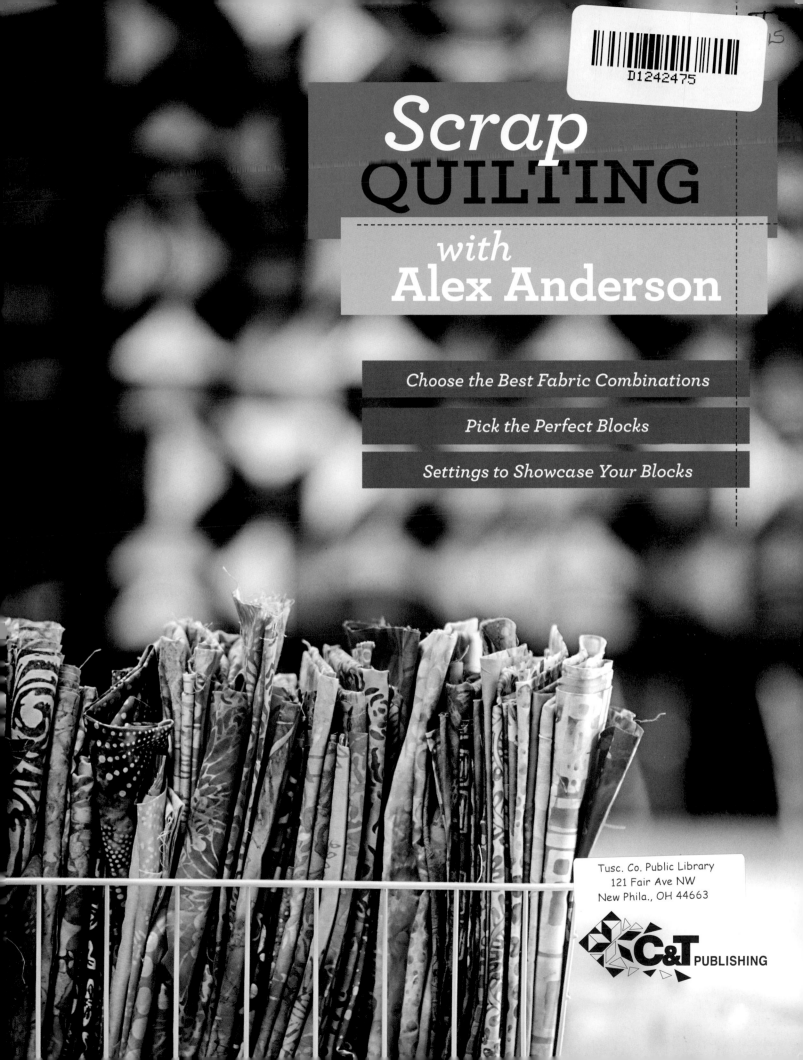

Scrap QUILTING

with Alex Anderson

- Choose the Best Fabric Combinations
- Pick the Perfect Blocks
- Settings to Showcase Your Blocks

C&T PUBLISHING

Publisher: Amy Marson

Creative Director: Gailen Runge

Art Director: Kristy Zacharias

Editor: Liz Aneloski

Technical Editors: Ellen Pahl and Gailen Runge

Cover Designer: Kristy Zacharias

Book Designer: Christina Jarumay Fox

Production Coordinators: Jenny Davis and Rue Flaherty

Production Editors: Joanna Burgarino and Katie Van Amburg

Illustrator: Jenny Davis

Photography by Diane Pedersen of C&T Publishing, Inc., unless
otherwise noted

Published by C&T Publishing, Inc., P.O. Box 1456, Lafayette, CA 94549

Library of Congress Cataloging-in-Publication Data

Anderson, Alex, 1955-

 Scrap quilting with Alex Anderson : choose the best fabric combinations - pick the perfect blocks - settings to showcase your blocks /
Alex Anderson.

  pages cm

 ISBN 978-1-60705-755-0 (soft cover)

1. Patchwork--Patterns. 2. Quilting--Patterns. I. Title.

 TT835.A493678 2013

 746.46--dc23

              2013002786

Printed in China

10 9 8 7 6 5 4 3 2 1

ACKNOWLEDGMENTS

My sincere thanks to

P&B Textiles, Westminster Fabrics, Robert Kaufman
Fabrics, LakeHouse Dry Goods, and Cherrywood Fabrics,
all of whom graciously provided wonderful fabric to
play with;

Bernina, for letting me play with and create using its
terrific sewing machines;

Bob and Heather Purcell of Superior Threads, for their
excellent products and their continued effort to educate
the masses about the wonderful world of thread;

Olfa Products, for great tools to work with;

Carolie Hensley at The Cotton Patch,
Lafayette, California, for her continued support;

Pam Vieira McGinnis, just for being there;

Erica von Holtz, for her eagle eye;

Carolyn Hughey, who understands it's all in the details;

and last but not least, Darra Williamson, who helps me
keep my ducks in a row!

DEDICATION

*This book would not have been possible
without the help of my two dear friends
and quilting buddies Darra Williamson and
Joen Wolfrom, who—after much debate
and discussion—helped me sort out
"What exactly defines a scrap quilt?"
and helped bring this idea to reality
at our annual retreat/escape.
Thank you, ladies. You are the best!*

CONTENTS

INTRODUCTION:

From One FABRIC LOVER to Another

I love my stash! I have spent many years building it, and it contains a delicious variety of "players." From lights to darks, polka dots to stripes, and beyond, my scrappy collection is always a source of inspiration to me.

So I guess it's natural that I love to make scrap quilts; I get to revisit all of my favorite fabrics and even—I'll admit it!—shop for more.

Besides getting to use a boatload of different fabrics, the thing I love most about making scrap quilts is the rule book. It's very short and sweet, and here it is:

The only rule for making a scrap quilt is that there are no rules.

That said, I do have lots of ideas about how to make a successful scrap quilt, and that's what this book is all about. For example, I tend to lean toward the simpler patterns and let the fusion of fabric take center stage. This is not the time for piecing gymnastics! You'll notice that the patterns I chose for the projects in this book fall into the easy-to-piece and not-too-many-pieces categories—Baskets, Bow Ties, Birds in the Air—and I hope you'll have fun making some of them yourself. But honestly? That's not the reason I wrote this book.

I know that making a scrap quilt—facing all those fabrics and making all those choices—can sometimes be a little overwhelming. Yes, some folks are lucky enough to do it intuitively, but some of us need a little structure. So what I've attempted to do here is to break the process down into manageable steps and to offer some useful guidelines for making color choices, for using your scraps and stash to good advantage, and for finding a design strategy that feels comfortable so that you can go beyond the quilts in this book to imagine and create some fabulous scrap quilts that are uniquely yours. You may find that you like maintaining a little control over the decisions that go into each block, or you might decide that the no-holds-barred approach is the way to go. It's all good, and I can almost guarantee, if you're making a scrap quilt, you're going to have fun.

And that's what it's all about, isn't it?

Scrap Quilt BASIC

What is a Scrap Quilt?

Now there's a good question. What *is* a scrap quilt? You could probably ask a dozen quilters to define the term *scrap quilt* and come up with a dozen different answers. Some would define a scrap quilt as a quilt made entirely from fabric leftovers. Some would say it's any quilt that incorporates a wide variety of fabrics or that partners different fabrics in each block ... and they're all correct. The definition of a scrap quilt is a pretty personal thing.

It's probably safe to say that my definition of a scrap quilt is a combination of the above. To me, a scrap quilt incorporates lots and lots of different fabrics; in fact, I challenge myself to get as many different fabrics into my scrap quilts as possible, and I challenge you to do the same. Sometimes I'll come up with a "formula" that places the lights and darks in the same position in the block for pretty much the entire quilt. (Note that I said *lights* and *darks*, not the same colors or fabrics.) Sometimes I'll mix things up and switch the lights and darks around from block to block. Sometimes, because the lightness or darkness of a fabric depends upon its relationship to its neighbors, I'll use the same fabric as a light in one block, a medium in another, and a dark in a third block.

Value—that is, the lightness or darkness of a fabric—is relative. The same fabric can play the role of a light, a medium, or a dark, depending upon its neighbors.

Sometimes I'll use a single background fabric to tie things together. Sometimes I'll use a different background fabric, or fabrics, in every block. And sometimes I just dive in and see what happens. As I said in the introduction, it's all good.

I also tend to interpret the term *scrap* kind of loosely. It's more a style than a thing. My scrap quilts might include a mix of small pieces left over from previous projects, pristine fat quarters waiting in my stash, or even fabric that I haven't purchased yet. The key is quantity, not where it came from.

If I impress one thought on you from the start, it's this: When you're making a scrap quilt, the focus is on the overall impression, the big picture, and not on every individual fabric or block. If you look closely at my quilts in this book (and many of those in the Gallery, page 62, too), you'll notice that not every fabric or block is a knockout. It's the mix that makes it work. Don't be afraid to work out of your comfort zone; a scrap quilt is much more forgiving than a quilt that uses just four or five fabrics, in which any misstep will be so much more obvious. Take a deep breath and pull out those what-was-I-thinking fabrics. You'll be cutting those challenging colors and prints into small pieces, and it's the blend that counts.

Examples of some challenging fabrics. Don't be afraid of them! They have the potential to make a quilt sing.

One more thought before we get down to serious play: Scrap quilts and contemporary quilts are not mutually exclusive! Yes, quilts made in traditional patterns from nineteenth-century reproduction fabrics or from the leftovers in Grandma's remnant bag may be scrap quilts, but so are quilts made using the latest, the brightest, the most trendy fabrics, as long as you use a lot of them. Traditional patterns like Sawtooth Star and Flying Geese can look brand new when dressed up in chic fabrics and showcased in sassy settings. So whether your taste is super traditional or cutting edge, you can satisfy your cravings with a scrap quilt.

Why Make a Scrap Quilt?

Chances are that if you're reading this book, you already have the itch to make a scrap quilt. It may be your first, or you may be an old hand looking for inspiration, motivation, or new strategies for approaching the process.

There are so many reasons to make a scrap quilt. The two most obvious are these:

You love the look, the unpredictability of a quilt with lots of different fabrics.

You have a large collection of fabric and scraps that you'd like to put to good use.

But there are lots of other reasons, some of which you might not have considered before and might bring a whole new dimension to the scrap-quilt experience:

Making a scrap quilt gives you the opportunity to evaluate and celebrate your fabric collection. Often we collect fabric without a specific purpose in mind, wash it when we get it home, fold it lovingly, place it on the shelf … and then forget we have it. In making a scrap quilt, you'll be pulling fabrics by the dozens from your stash to consider for a project. Who knows what forgotten treasures you might rediscover?

Personally, I love this excuse to reconnect with my stash and relive the memories of how this or that fabric found its way into my collection. We quilters come by our fabric in so many different ways, and making a scrap quilt is a lovely way to revisit those people, places, and life experiences. In the end, a scrap quilt tells a story about you. It's filled with lovely little secrets about who you are, where you've been, and so much more. It connects you to those who view the quilt, especially other quilters who might recognize some of the fabrics you've used and be inspired by how you've used them.

A scrap quilt is a quilt that keeps on giving, drawing the viewer in, revealing itself slowly, and continually surprising with new discoveries. It's impossible to take it all in with a single glance, so it retains its mystery much longer than a quilt that repeats the same four or five fabrics from block to block.

Another bonus to working with scraps is that the design process is flexible. Nothing is set in stone from the start, so you can continue to edit the quilt as you go. Blocks looking too dull? Pep them up by mixing in a few spicy neighbors, or introduce a lively print for the setting blocks or sashing. Quilt running wild? Pop in a few quiet, low-contrast blocks, or give those party boys some breathing space with soothing tone-on-tone alternate blocks. The process is fun, fun, fun— and full of surprises—from beginning to end.

Making a scrap quilt will help you grow as a quiltmaker. If you've always restricted yourself to just four or five fabrics and have always planned every detail of a quilt before cutting the first fabric, your first few scrappy blocks may be rather timid. However, as the scrappy blocks roll off your sewing machine, chances are you'll find yourself becoming more adventurous and your confidence will begin to grow. With time, you'll find yourself able to pick up almost any piece of fabric and find a way to work it into a scrap quilt.

Are you ready? Let's get started.

Fabric Strategies

Photo by Alex Anderson

I'm sure you've heard some variation of the expression "The person with the most fabric wins." While this makes for a clever bumper sticker, I prefer to say that it's not necessarily the person with the *biggest* stash, but the person with the *healthiest* stash who wins.

Three Keys to a Healthy Stash

It's a good idea to evaluate your stash from time to time to see if there are any serious gaps in your inventory. In fact, I highly recommend it, especially if you plan to make scrap quilts.

What makes a healthy stash? To me, it's a fabric collection that's well rounded, one that includes a good mix of color, value, and character of print.

COLOR

Were you to ask most quilters the first thing that attracts them to a particular fabric, they'd probably say color. Most of us have our favorites, the ones we're drawn to and buy over and over again. Good for the soul, but not necessarily the best thing for a scrap quilter's stash.

If you look at old quilts, particularly scrap quilts, you'll often discover colors or combinations of colors that would never cross your mind as candidates for your next quilting project.

Our foremothers (and occasionally, forefathers) were fearless; they worked with rich red, electric blue, bile green, bubble-gum pink, cheddar orange—sometimes all in the same quilt—and we're still admiring these quilts 125-plus years later.

Even if your taste leans toward a less traditional look, there are lessons to be learned from these vintage beauties. Don't be afraid to open yourself to *all* the colors available to you, not just the ones that you love and that you've always worked with before. As you continue to grow your fabric stash, keep an eye out for the colors that are missing from the collection, and make a note to hunt them down next time you head to your favorite fabric source. Your future scrap quilts will love you for it!

▶▶ *tip*

All in the (Color) Family

When we speak of a color, we're speaking of that color's *entire family*—and color families can be quite large. They include all the lights and darks, tints and shades of that particular family.

VALUE

Value refers to the relative lightness or darkness of a fabric, and you'll want to be certain that you have a good range of values—light to dark—of every color in your stash. It's what transforms a color into a color family.

The key word in that definition is *relative*. You can't tell how light or dark a fabric is when you look at it by itself. It all depends upon the other fabrics that surround it in the block or quilt.

It's often been said that "color gets the credit, but value does work." In my book, it's true, true, true!

For example, in a Star block, the star points define the star image. Place the fabric with the strongest contrast in value—say, the darkest fabric—in the star-point position, and there'll be no missing the intent. On the other hand, place that dark fabric in the center of the star, and that's where the eye will go. Set a bunch of these blocks together, and the Star quilt will read as a sea of big, dark squares.

With this principle in mind, my basic plan for *Seeing Stars* (page 45) was to make the star tips darker than the star centers in every block. Even though some of those star-point fabrics are not super dark, they are always *relatively* darker than the fabrics I used for the star centers and background, so the stars come shining through.

Detail of *Seeing Stars* (page 45). Even when the contrast in the fabrics is low, the relative darkness of the star points defines the star image.

CHARACTER OF PRINT

Character of print refers to the figures or motifs that appear on a printed fabric. (Some quilters call this "visual texture"—same thing.) As with color and value, you'll want your fabric collection to include a good mix of prints. The varieties shown here will give your stash a sound foundation.

FLORALS

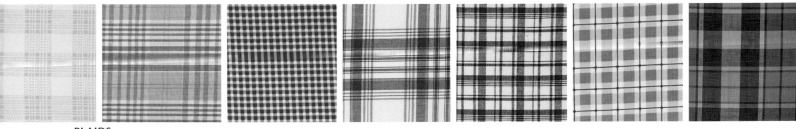

PLAIDS

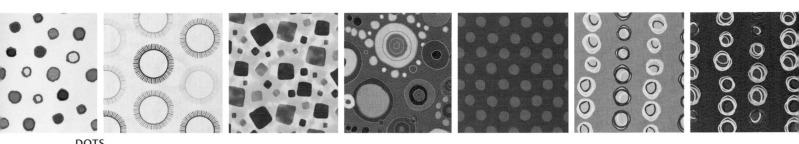

DOTS

FEATHERS AND PAISLEYS

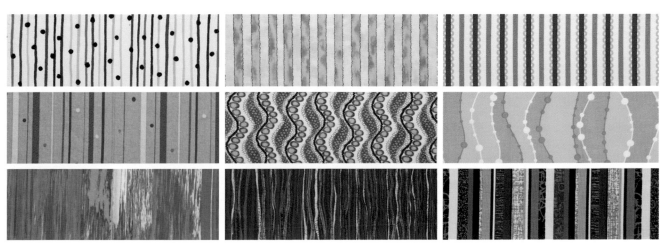

STRIPES

PICTURE PRINTS

ORGANICS/FOLIAGE

NATURE'S BOUNTY

SWIRLS AND TWIRLS

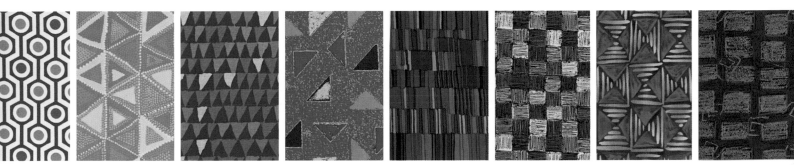

GEOMETRICS

As you diversify your stash with a variety of prints, remember that the old adage "You can't judge a book by its cover" can apply to fabric, too. Don't be afraid of large-scale and otherwise unusual designs. You'll be cutting these fabrics into small pieces, and the results can be surprising. A window template, tailored to the size and shape of the piece you'll be cutting, will give you a good preview.

A window template gives a good idea of how a large-scale or otherwise unusual print will look when cut into small pieces.

▶▶ *tip*

Add Some Sparkle

Before we move on, I want to put in a word for what I call "sparkle" fabrics. Sparkle fabrics are monochromatic prints that include the complete range of value—light to dark—of their particular color family; sometimes they include bits of white as well. You'll love the crispness these lively prints give to a scrap quilt.

"Sparkle" fabrics add personality and visual texture to a scrap quilt.

Why Shop for a Scrap Quilt?

If you're one of those lucky quilters who already has a healthy stash of fabric and scraps, you may be wondering why you'd want to add to your collection. Perhaps the most obvious reason is that you're a quilter. New fabrics continue to appear in the marketplace, and we quilters *do* love the new stuff! Colors and styles come and go, and it's always a good idea to take advantage of opportunities when we see them. An infusion of even a few trendy colors and prints can add freshness to a quilt. Just because it's a "scrap" quilt doesn't mean it doesn't deserve at least a *little* new fabric.

There are many ways to sort and store fabrics: by color, by style, by era (nineteenth-century reproductions, 1930s prints), by use (focus or border fabrics), even by designer. Be creative and find the method that works best for you.

HOW MUCH TO BUY

I'm always on the lookout for fabrics to expand and enrich my stash, and when I find something I like or that I know will fill a gap in my collection, I buy at least ⅓ yard. If I find a print that has the potential to become the foundation for a quilt—for example, a promising focus fabric (page 20)—I guesstimate enough for a border, and then add an additional ½ yard, just in case. (If nothing else, I know I can use the yardage for backing.)

When determining your own shopping guidelines, budget and storage space will, of course, come into play. You'll also want to consider the size quilts you usually make. A quilter who leans toward king- or queen-size projects will probably buy more fabric—either in variety or quantity—than one who rarely makes anything larger than a wall quilt.

When is a scrap too small to keep? Since I took a class with Susan Carlson, a fabric collage artist, no scrap is too tiny for me to keep.

Fabric as a Starting Point

So … now that you've got a healthy fabric stash—or are on the way to building one—it's time to put that fabric to work to make some scrumptious scrap quilts. Where to begin? Here are some suggestions.

WORK THE COLOR WHEEL

Whenever I'm stumped for a color scheme or wonder if the colors I'm considering for a quilt will play well together, I look to the color wheel. I also pull it out if I feel my palette would benefit from the addition of another color (or colors). It's a terrific little tool and a great guide for determining successful color relationships, especially when you're expanding your horizons to work with colors you might not have worked with before. Photocopy the color wheel on page 80 onto cardstock and use it to help make your color decisions.

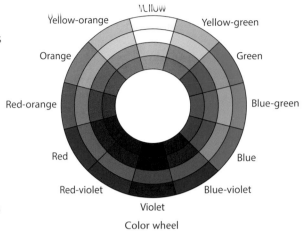

Color wheel

While I won't go into a lot of color theory, I feel that a few general principles might be helpful. Here are some basic color schemes that you can draw from the color wheel.

■ **Monochromatic:** This color scheme showcases a single color family in all its glory; for example, a blue color scheme can include blues from the palest baby blue to deep, rich navy.

Monochromatic color scheme

■ **Complementary:** This color scheme is built around two color families that appear opposite each other on the color wheel—for example, red and green.

Complementary color scheme

■ **Triadic:** This color scheme is built around three color families that are equally distant from each other on the wheel, such as yellow-orange, red-violet, and blue-green. To find a triadic color scheme, start with a single color on the wheel and, moving clockwise, skip three colors, select the next, skip three more, and select the next color, too. Repeat and you're back to the starting point. See how each Shoo Fly block uses a triadic color scheme? Bingo: a perfect triadic color scheme!

Triadic color scheme

■ **Analogous:** This color scheme is made up of neighbors on the color wheel, and it can include three, four, or more side-by-side color families. This is one of the easiest and most relaxing schemes to work with, as each color contains some element of its immediate neighbors and the colors flow seamlessly one to the next.

Analogous color scheme

FIND A FABULOUS FOCUS FABRIC

A focus fabric is a multicolored, often large-scale print that you can build a color scheme—and a quilt—around. In short, the fabric designer has done the heavy lifting for you! Study the colors in the focus fabric, pull a wide variety of fabrics in those colors from your stash, check that they include a good range of value and of character of print, and you're ready to go. How easy is that?

My focus fabric for *Baskets* (page 36) was the large-scale multicolored print that I used for the border.

SHOWCASE A DESIGNER

Every once in a while, a designer comes along whose fabrics just speak to me, and I find myself adding more and more of that designer's pieces to my stash. Over time, that area of my collection grows to include vintage pieces from that designer's various fabric lines as well as his or her newest creations.

My guess is that you have favorite designers (or fabric lines) too … and they make another great starting point for a super scrap quilt.

I sometimes use fabrics from a single designer—in the case of *Seeing Stars* (page 45), Kaffe Fassett—even when making a scrap quilt. I just use lots of them!

CAPTURE A STYLE OR AN ERA

Given my love for vintage quilts, it's not surprising that some of my favorite scrap quilts to make are those that replicate the look or style of a particular time period. With so many luscious reproduction fabrics available, it's fun—and easy—to make a quilt that looks as though it were fashioned in the nineteenth century or created during the height of the 1930s quilt revival.

Scrappy Sampler (page 57) was built around my treasured stash of nineteenth-century reproduction fabrics.

ALL'S FAIR IN LOVE … AND SCRAP QUILTS

If you're feeling particularly adventurous, throw caution to the wind and mine your entire stash to build a scrap quilt. Tap the rainbow. Mix different styles and scales of print. Trust your instincts. Glorious adventure awaits!

Time to start stitching. The next chapter will give you a variety of strategies for turning those fabrics you've collected into super scrappy quilts.

Design and Construction Strategies

Frequently, when I start thinking about making a new quilt, I turn to the books in my quilting library with lots of photos of antique quilts. (Confession time: I have many of these books, and they are very well used!) Over time, I've learned to look closely, really closely, to identify the details that make those particular quilts so appealing to me.

One thing I've discovered is that, in many cases, these "traditional" quilts were more renegade, and frankly often more interesting, than what many consider to be traditional quilts today. There was a freshness and freedom in these vintage quilts that I find very exciting.

I love the quirky features in old quilts and use them frequently in the quilts I'm making today, adapting brilliant nineteenth-century innovations to my twenty-first-century quilts. This chapter explains how I do it.

Getting Started

As I mentioned, I often use my books of antique quilts to generate ideas for beginning a new project. When that new project will be a scrap quilt, I keep my eyes open for blocks that are fairly simple. Four-Patches, Nine-Patches, Star variations, Log Cabins, Churn Dash, Flying Geese—with their easy construction and limited number of pieces, these old favorites are perfect for the scrap treatment, and I'm always amazed at how fresh and new they can look.

I prefer to keep the blocks for my scrappy quilts on the smallish side, generally 4" or 6", depending upon the number of pieces. Sometimes I'll go as large as 10" for a more complex block, but that's the exception rather than the rule. If the pieces get too big, my preferred simple blocks begin to look clunky.

Some of my favorites are blocks that are split on the diagonal, with the potential to make one half of the block light and the other half dark. The block can be as simple as the half-square triangle (see Kim McCloskey's *Kuleidoscope*, page 71), or a little more involved, such as Birds in the Air. You can place these divided blocks in dozens of different arrangements—think Log Cabin—and never come up with the same look twice.

Blocks that divide on the diagonal, such as those in *Birds in the Air* (page 41), add movement and excitement to a quilt's surface.

Simple blocks work best for busy scrap quilts. I used the *Quick & Easy Block Tool* to select the blocks for my quilts in this book (see Resources, page 79).

Block Strategies

There are many different ways you can approach making the blocks for a scrap quilt, depending upon your personal taste, your level of confidence (make that fearlessness), the size of your fabric collection, and even the size of the pieces in your collection. Here are a few possibilities to consider, keeping in mind that a plan is just a starting point and can be altered at any time in the scrap-quilt process.

- ☐ Use a consistent fabric throughout for the block backgrounds, changing the fabrics that make up the design (for example, Star, Churn Dash) in each block. The background can be light, dark, or medium in value.

- ☐ Use two (or more) fabrics for the backgrounds in each block.

- ☐ Make every block from two or three fabrics that play nicely together, maintaining the basic placement of value but changing up the fabrics from block to block.

- ☐ Go completely random, using and mixing up multiple fabrics in each block.

Two-fabric block

Dark backgrounds

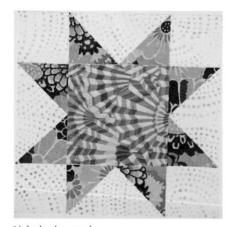

Light background

Multiple background fabrics

Making the Blocks

Once you've assembled the fabrics, chosen the block (or blocks), and decided on a basic fabric strategy, it's time to start sewing.

I often start my scrap quilts without a clue about how the blocks will be arranged in the final setting, whether there will be sashing or alternate blocks, or how I will handle any other major design decisions. Sometimes I'll have a loose plan—based around a focus fabric that I'm considering for a border, for example—but even that's subject to change as the blocks begin to pile up beside my sewing machine.

It may seem a little scary at first, to begin cutting and sewing blocks without a sketch of the finished quilt in front of you or pictured inside your head, or without the sashing or border fabric chosen beforehand. I have a feeling, though, that as you get into the process, you'll begin to relax and surrender happily to the fun and excitement of seeing how the quilt develops.

Here's my usual game plan.

1. Make a block, and then another block, and then another. Don't look back, and don't second-guess yourself. It's way too early in the game. Just keep moving forward!

 tip

Ever Onward!

If it takes you ten minutes to decide which fabric to use in the next block, you're thinking too much! Trust your instincts. Choose, sew, and move on.

2. Consider each block to be an independent marcher. Don't worry about the blocks matching each other. Still too early.

3. Don't panic if not every block is "pretty." When you're making a scrap quilt, it's the big picture, not the individual fabric or block that matters … and sometimes it's the blocks with personality that put a smile on your face. If a particular block is still bugging you further on down the road, you can always pull it out. (I can tell you from experience: Chances are, you won't.)

Not every block will be a beauty queen, but that's OK!

MAVERICK BLOCKS

Let's take a moment to talk a bit more about those quirky "personality" blocks. They're the mavericks, the ones that don't necessarily follow the rules, but—as in life—they often turn out to be the life of the party.

In many older quilts, it's not unusual to find that although the same block or blocks are repeated throughout, the placement of the values (light, medium, and dark) within the blocks varies considerably. Sometimes it's a challenge to recognize that two differently shaded blocks are made from the same pieces. For example, the familiar Sawtooth Star block can take on many different looks,

depending upon how the values are placed. As long as there are enough blocks that announce "Sawtooth Star," the quilt will "read" as a Star quilt.

It may be a stretch for you to break the rules, but it can be a very freeing experience and one that greatly expands your skills as a quiltmaker. It can also be a very, *very* good thing for a quilt.

A few oddball or maverick blocks can add lots of personality to a scrap quilt.

When you make that first maverick block, it will look very strange and out of place; after all, it's the one oddball among the conformers. Don't panic! As you make a few more—not too many, just a few—and add them to the mix, that maverick won't be quite so jarring and will likely fit in just fine. The end result is a visually appealing, vibrant quilt that keeps the eye moving and the viewer engaged.

Evaluating Your Progress

Once you've made a bunch of blocks, it's time to put them on a design wall and assess what you've got. This is when the quilt will really begin to speak to you, to make its needs and preferences known—and it's always a good idea to listen. Are the blocks looking too "samey"? Try mixing in a few mavericks. Blocks running wild? Maybe a few predictable, easy-to-read, high-contrast blocks are what you need. Is there a single oddball block or color jumping out at you? Make a few more blocks, repeating that stand-out element, and spread them out so they flow seamlessly into the mix. The eye will absorb these mavericks along with the rest of the blocks (big picture, remember?) as it skims the surface of the quilt, reading the design from the majority of the blocks, the ones that follow the rules.

Here's an example of how easy it is to edit a scrap quilt in progress. As I began placing the blocks for *Seeing Stars* (page 45) on my design wall, I realized that some of the star centers (or "star bellies," as I like to call them) were *way* too dark, calling too much attention to themselves, weighing things down. As I continued to make the additional blocks I needed for the quilt top, I focused on shifting the balance back to my original formula of dark point and medium center, and I introduced airy polka dot prints for some of those star bellies. I sprinkled the new, less weighty blocks into the mix—problem solved!

Star block with a heavy belly

▶▶ tip

The Indispensable Design Wall

I can't imagine making a quilt without a design wall. My design wall is as essential to me as my rotary cutter and sewing machine.

Seeing Stars (page 45) in progress on my design wall

Photo by Alex Anderson

Not everyone has the luxury of open wall space in the sewing room for a permanent design surface, but there are many options. One of my favorites is to cover one side of a large piece—for example, 4′ × 6′—of foam core or wallboard with flannel or felt, wrap the excess to the back of the board, and pin or staple to secure. You can prop this portable design board against a wall, door, or large piece of furniture while you're working, and slip it under a bed for storage when you're not.

▶▶ tip

Going to Plan B

There may be times when a block or two just won't fit, no matter how hard you try. Don't be afraid to remove it from the wall. You can always set it aside for a future project or—better still—incorporate it into the backing of the quilt you're making.

Star block with a better belly

Setting Options

Once you've got a healthy number of blocks on the design wall, it's time to consider how to arrange them to create the quilt top. There are loads of options, and the best thing to do is to experiment. Try shifting, staggering, rotating the blocks. In some cases, you'll discover wonderful surprises.

Here are just a few of the possibilities you can try.

☐ **Block-to-block setting:** For this simple setting, blocks are set together with their edges touching.

☐ **Alternate-block (or sashed) setting:** Inserting plain blocks or sashing strips between the pieced blocks is a good option if you feel the quilt needs some breathing space. The addition of cornerstones introduces another possibility for secondary design.

Sometimes wonderful secondary designs appear when blocks are rotated, as I discovered while playing with the blocks for *Birds in the Air* (page 41).

Detail of *Shoo Fly Variation* (page 53), a block-to-block setting; other examples include *Bow Ties* (page 32) and *Birds in the Air* (page 41)

Detail of *Universe* (page 72), with plain blocks between the pieced blocks, giving the eye a place to rest

☐ **On-point (or diagonal) setting:**
Many a block takes on a whole new
personality when turned on its ear.
This is particularly true of blocks made
completely from squares, such as the
Four-Patch and Nine-Patch. Others,
such as Basket and Tree blocks, seem
naturally designed to be set that way.

Don't let the orientation of the blocks
throw you. They are sewn together as
usual, but with this setting the rows
are finished with side and corner
setting triangles to square up the quilt
center—another opportunity to add
fun fabrics to the mix.

Detail of *Baskets* (page 36), an on-point (or diagonal) setting

☐ **Strippy setting:** In this setting,
blocks are arranged in vertical (or
horizontal) rows with strips of fabric
in between. Blocks can be set straight
or on point, as Diana McClun and
Laura Nownes did in *Sensu* (page 68).
You might even piece those setting
strips (Flying Geese are fun) or add
appliquéd vines or other simple motifs.

Detail of *Sensu* (page 68), with on-point blocks set in vertical rows

■ **Randomly staggered setting:** Blocks don't need to line up in perfect rows, nor do they need to be the same size, although it does help to choose blocks that are mathematically compatible—for example, blocks that can be divided into units or increments of 2″. If necessary, you can use filler strips or squares to fill the gaps. Just be sure to divide things up so that you can sew larger sections—or neighborhoods—together with straight-line seams, as I did with *Seeing Stars* (page 45) and *Scrappy Sampler* (page 57).

▶▶ *tips*

Troubleshooting Tips for Successful Settings

□ If you have a block with a what-was-I-thinking fabric or color, offset it—in the lower left-hand quarter of the setting, for example—and then repeat that fabric or color in two other blocks, scattering them elsewhere around the quilt.

□ Grouping the darker blocks in the bottom half of the setting grounds a quilt and gives it weight, with the lighter blocks above appearing free to float away. Reverse this arrangement— darker blocks on top, lighter on the bottom—and the quilt may seem top-heavy, trapping those lighter blocks below.

□ Here's a little tip I learned from friend and quilter Diana McClun. Place high-contrast blocks in the four corners of a scrap quilt top to reinforce the design. *Baskets* (page 36) is a good example.

Detail of *Seeing Stars* (page 45), a staggered setting with filler blocks and strips

I mixed blocks of different sizes in *Scrappy Sampler* (page 57). All were easily divisible by 2″.

Adding Borders

Who says that every quilt must have four borders? That all border strips must be cut from the same fabric and to the same width? That these strips must be (choose one) wholecloth, pieced, or appliquéd?

Not every quilt needs a border; in many vintage scrap quilts, the blocks spill right to the edges, with no frame at all, and the results are just fine. I sometimes choose this option, but with a twist, reversing the values in the outer rows of blocks to create a faux border with these contrasting blocks.

Carolyn Hughey opted for multiple unpieced borders on her quilt *Shoo Fly Variation* (page 53) before adding a pieced finale.

By changing the placement of value within the blocks, I created the illusion of a border in *Bow Ties* (page 32).

For some scrap quilts, if one border is good, why not two or three? In her *Shoo Fly Variation* (page 53), Carolyn Hughey surrounded the quilt center with four borders, three plain and one pieced. Notice that she picked up and repeated the triangle shape in the outermost border to tie it back to the quilt center.

When I plan multiple borders for one of my scrap quilts, I'll often use a narrow border of striped fabric for the innermost frame. I love the way the stripe holds the busy quilt center together, especially when a second, pieced border is to follow.

I inserted a narrow border on just two sides of *Scrappy Sampler* (page 57) to allow some space between the blocks ... and to help the math work out right!

Thoughts on Quilting

Good quilting design doesn't just happen. Planning is essential, and being able to recognize a successful design—one that complements rather than competes, that supports rather than detracts—is essential as well.

With a scrap quilt's generous mix of printed fabrics, it's pretty unlikely that elaborate quilting motifs will show to best advantage on its heavily pieced areas. Save those fancy wreaths, feathers, and other complex quilting designs for solids, tone-on-tones, and lightly patterned prints, and for filling the more open areas on a quilt—such as plain alternate blocks or sashing or plain borders—where every beautiful stitch will be seen. For densely pieced or printed areas, keep it simple. Don't be afraid to cross the lines. When it comes to planning quilting designs, especially for scrap quilts, seamlines are arbitrary. Overall patterns such as grids, fans, and even some unfussy cables work well here; the repetitive pattern is easily recognized, so the brain fills in the blanks. Another option is to follow the design on the printed fabric, which will add texture without adding additional pattern. Mine the focus fabric for overall design ideas.

Here are some additional guidelines for quilting a scrap quilt. (In fact, these are good things to keep in mind when designing a quilting plan for *any* quilt.)

☐ **Fill the space.** Just as you wouldn't want to jam a huge house on a postage-stamp lot, you'll want to make sure that the amount of quilting in your plan is appropriate for the area of the quilt that you're aiming to fill. Not enough quilting, and the space looks awkward and empty, as though you underplanned, became bored, or ran out of time and energy. Too much quilting, and the piece can look cramped.

☐ **Distribute quilting evenly over the entire surface of the quilt.** Think balance. If you fill some areas with heavy quilting and then skimp on other areas, the finished quilt not only will look unbalanced but will be inclined to both sag unattractively in the underquilted spots and pucker where the sparsely and densely quilted areas meet.

☐ **Mix curves with geometry and geometry with curves.** Gently curved fans, feathers, and cables soften the straight lines and sharp angles of many of our favorite geometric blocks. The opposite also holds true: Straight lines make a nice visual counterpoint to curvy, organic appliqué shapes.

Detail of *Shoo Fly Variation* (page 53). Overall patterns, such as crosshatched quilting, are often fine choices for scrap quilts.

Curved lines of quilting make a nice complement to the geometry of the blocks in the border of *Bow Ties* (page 32).

IT'S
PLAY

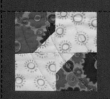

Bow Ties

Designed and pieced by Alex Anderson. Machine quilted by Dianne Schweickert.

As *Bow Ties* was growing on my design wall, I wasn't sure what to do about a border, or if the quilt even needed one. As so often happens, I just kept working and eventually the solution seemed plain as could be, almost as if the quilt had spoken to me. I made a series of blocks in which I changed the placement of the light and dark values and arranged these blocks in a double row around the quilt's outer edges. The contrast was just enough to create the illusion of a border—just the subtle touch the quilt needed.

Finished quilt size: 56½″ × 56½″

Finished block size: 4″ × 4″

Total number of Bow Tie blocks: 196

- **Block 1:** 100

- **Block 2:** 96

Skill level: *Confident beginner*

MATERIALS

Fabric amounts are based on a 42″ fabric width.

Assorted light prints: 2¼ yards total for blocks

Assorted medium to dark prints: 2¼ yards total for blocks

Dark brown print: ½ yard for binding

Backing: 3½ yards of fabric

Batting: 61″ × 61″ piece

CUTTING

All measurements include ¼″-wide seam allowance. Cutting is given for a single block. Cut as you go, or cut the total number given in parentheses. Cut strips on the crosswise grain of the fabric (selvage to selvage). See the introductions to Block 1 and Block 2 (page 34) for the number and combination of pieces you'll use for each block.

BOW TIE BLOCK 1 (100 TOTAL)

From 1 light print

- Cut 2 squares 2½″ × 2½″ for the background (200).

From 1 medium/dark print

- Cut 2 squares 2½″ × 2½″ (200).

- Cut 2 squares 1½″ × 1½″ (200).

BOW TIE BLOCK 2 (96 TOTAL)

From 1 light print

- Cut 2 squares 2½″ × 2½″ (192).

- Cut 2 squares 1½″ × 1½″ (192).

From 1 medium/dark print

- Cut 2 squares 2½″ × 2½″ (192).

BINDING

From the dark brown print

- Cut 6 strips 2⅛″ × the fabric width.

PIECING THE BLOCKS

Make a total of 196 Bow Tie blocks for this quilt: 100 of Block 1 (dark bow tie with lighter background) and 96 of Block 2 (light bow tie with darker background).

BLOCK 1

For each Block 1, use 2 matching light print squares 2½" × 2½" for the background and 2 matching pairs of darker print squares, 2½" × 2½" and 1½" × 1½", for the bow tie. These blocks are for the center of the quilt.

1. Draw a diagonal line from corner to corner on the wrong side of the 2 matching medium/dark 1½" × 1½" squares. Align a marked square, right sides together, with a corner of a light 2½" × 2½" square; pin. Repeat to prepare 2 units.

Make 2.

2. Sew directly on the marked lines. Trim the seam allowances to ¼". Press the seams toward the darker fabric. Make 2.

Make 2.

3. Arrange the units from Step 2 with 2 matching darker 2½" × 2½" squares. Sew the units and squares together in pairs; press. Sew the pairs together; press.

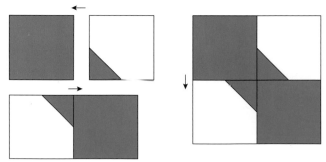

Sew units and squares together in pairs.

4. Repeat Steps 1–3 to make 100 of Block 1.

BLOCK 2

For each Block 2, use 2 matching medium/dark print 2½" × 2½" squares for the background and 2 matching pairs of light print squares, 2½" × 2½" and 1½" × 1½", for the bow tie. These blocks are for the "border" of the quilt.

1. Draw a diagonal line from corner to corner on the wrong side of the 2 matching light 1½" × 1½" squares. Align a marked square, right sides together, with a corner of a darker 2½" × 2½" square; pin. Repeat to prepare 2 units.

Make 2.

2. Sew directly on the marked lines. Trim seams to ¼". Press toward the darker fabric. Make 2.

Make 2.

3. Arrange the units from Step 2 with 2 matching light 2½" × 2½" squares. Sew the units and squares together in pairs; press. Sew the pairs together; press.

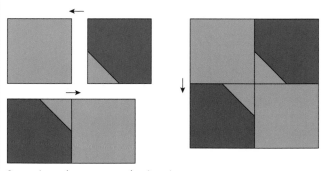

Sew units and squares together in pairs.

4. Repeat Steps 1–3 to make 96 of Block 2.

QUILT ASSEMBLY

1. Arrange Blocks 1 in 10 horizontal rows of 10 blocks each to form the quilt center, turning the blocks as shown in the assembly diagram

2. Arrange Blocks 2 around the outer edges of the quilt center, turning the blocks as shown in the assembly diagram.

3. Sew the blocks together into rows. Press seams in alternating directions from row to row. Sew the rows together; press.

FINISHING

Refer to Finishing Your Quilt (page 77).

1. Layer and baste the quilt, and then quilt as desired. Dianne machine quilted a crosshatched grid over the center of the quilt and a wide cable in the outer border.

2. Sew the 2⅛"-wide dark brown print strips together end to end with diagonal seams, and use them to bind the edges.

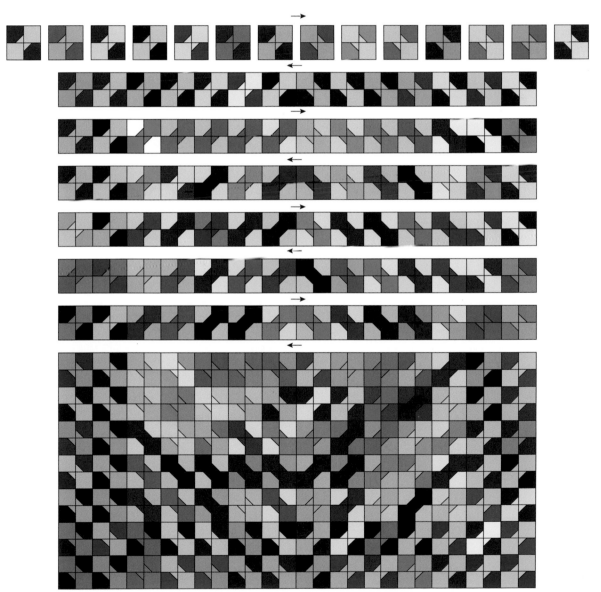

Assembly diagram

Baskets

Designed and pieced by Alex Anderson. Machine quilted by Diana Johnson.

Choosing a color scheme for this quilt was soooo easy! I started with the large-scale border print as the focus fabric and I used its color cues to guide the selection of fabrics for the basket blocks. I repeated the same large-scale print for the setting triangles, which helped to further integrate the blocks with the border. I think it worked out very nicely, don't you?

Finished quilt size: 59″ × 59″

Finished block size: 6″ × 6″

Total number of Basket blocks: 41

- ■ **Block 1:** 25

- ■ **Block 2:** 16

Skill level: *Confident beginner*

MATERIALS

Fabric amounts are based on a 42″ fabric width.

Assorted light prints: 1½ yards total for blocks

Assorted dark prints: 1½ yards total for blocks

Assorted medium prints: ⅔ yard total for blocks

Large-scale floral print: 1¾ yards for setting triangles and outer border

Light stripe: ⅜ yard for inner border

Dark purple print: ½ yard for binding

Backing: 3⅝ yards of fabric

Batting: 63″ × 63″ piece

CUTTING

All measurements include ¼″-wide seam allowance. Cutting is given for a single block. Cut as you go, or cut the total number given in parentheses. Cut strips on the crosswise grain of the fabric (selvage to selvage) unless otherwise noted. See the introductions to Block 1 (page 38) and Block 2 (page 39) for the number and combination of pieces you'll use for each block.

BASKET BLOCK 1 (25 TOTAL)

From 1 light print

- ☐ Cut 2 squares 2⅜″ × 2⅜″ (50 total); cut each square in half once diagonally to make 4 half-square triangles.

- ☐ Cut 1 square 2″ × 2″ (25).

- ☐ Cut 2 rectangles 2″ × 3½″ (50).

- ☐ Cut 1 square 3⅞″ × 3⅞″ (25 total); cut the square in half once diagonally to make 2 half-square triangles (1 is extra).

From 1 dark print

- ☐ Cut 3 squares 2⅜″ × 2⅜″ (75 total); cut each square in half once diagonally to make 6 half-square triangles.

- ☐ Cut 1 square 3⅞″ × 3⅞″ (25 total); cut the square in half once diagonally to make 2 half-square triangles (1 is extra).

From 1 medium print

- ☐ Cut 1 square 3⅞″ × 3⅞″ (25 total); cut the square in half once diagonally to make 2 half-square triangles (1 is extra).

BASKET BLOCK 2 (16 TOTAL)

From 1 light print

- ☐ Cut 3 squares 2⅜″ × 2⅜″ (48 total); cut each square in half once diagonally to make 6 half-square triangles.

- ☐ Cut 1 square 3⅞″ × 3⅞″ (16 total); cut the square in half once diagonally to make 2 half-square triangles (1 is extra).

From 1 dark print

- ☐ Cut 2 squares 2⅜″ × 2⅜″ (32 total); cut each square in half once diagonally to make 4 half-square triangles.

- ☐ Cut 1 square 2″ × 2″ (16).

- ☐ Cut 2 rectangles 2″ × 3½″ (32).

- ☐ Cut 1 square 3⅞″ × 3⅞″ (16 total); cut the square in half once diagonally to make 2 half-square triangles (1 is extra).

From 1 medium print

■ Cut 1 square 3⅞" × 3⅞" (16 total); cut the square in half once diagonally to make 2 half-square triangles (1 is extra).

SETTING TRIANGLES, BORDERS, AND BINDING

From the *lengthwise grain* of the large-scale floral print

■ Cut 2 strips 7" × 46".

■ Cut 2 strips 7" × 59".

From the remaining large-scale floral print

■ Cut 4 squares 9¾" × 9¾"; cut each square in half twice diagonally to make a total of 16 quarter-square side setting triangles.

■ Cut 2 squares 5⅛" × 5⅛"; cut each square in half once diagonally to make a total of 4 half-square corner setting triangles.

From the light stripe

■ Cut 5 strips 2" × the fabric width.

From the dark purple print

■ Cut 7 strips 2⅛" × the fabric width.

PIECING THE BLOCKS

Make a total of 41 Basket blocks: 25 of Block 1 (dark basket with lighter background) and 16 of Block 2 (light basket with darker background).

BLOCK 1

For each of these blocks, use 4 half-square triangles 2⅜", a square 2" × 2", a pair of rectangles 2" × 3½", and a half-square triangle 3⅞", all cut from the same light print, for the background. Use 6 half-square triangles 2⅜" and a half-square triangle 3⅞", all cut from the same dark print, for the basket. Use a medium print half-square triangle 3⅞" for the basket "filling."

1. Sew a light triangle 2⅜" and a dark triangle 2⅜" together along their long edges. Press the seam toward the darker triangle. Make 4 matching units.

Make 4.

2. Sew 2 units from Step 1 in pairs; press. Make 1 of each as shown.

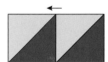

Make 1 each.

3. Sew a unit from Step 2 to a short side of a medium triangle 3⅞"; press.

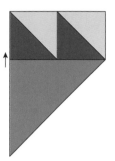

Sew unit to short side of triangle.

4. Sew a light 2" × 2" square to the remaining unit from Step 2; press. Sew this to the unit from Step 3; press.

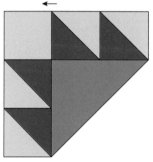

Sew square to unit; sew units together.

5. Sew a dark 3⅞" triangle to the unit from Step 4; press.

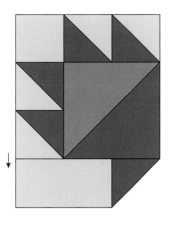

Sew triangle to unit.

6. Sew a dark triangle 2⅜" to an end of a light 2" × 3½" rectangle; press. Make 1 of each as shown.

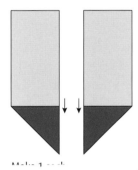

7. Sew the units from Step 6 to the unit from Step 5; press.

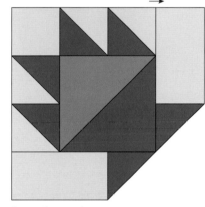

Sew units together.

8. Sew a light triangle 3⅞" to the bottom of the unit from Step 7; press.

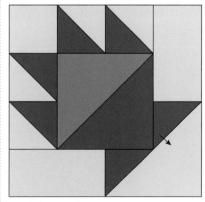

Sew light triangle to unit.

9. Repeat Steps 1–8 to make 25 total of Block 1.

BLOCK 2

For each of these blocks, use 4 half-square triangles 2⅜", a square 2" × 2", a pair of rectangles 2" × 3½", and a half-square triangle 3⅞", all cut from the same dark print, for the background. Use 6 half-square triangles 2⅜" and a half-square triangle 3⅞", all cut from the same light print, for the basket. Use a medium print half-square triangle 3⅞" for the basket filling.

Refer to Block 1, Steps 1–8, reversing the placement of the light and dark pieces. Make a total of 16 of Block 2.

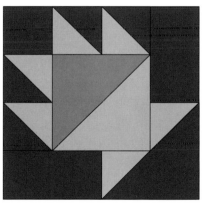

Make 16.

QUILT ASSEMBLY

1. Arrange Blocks 1 and 2, the quarter-square side setting triangles, and the half-square corner setting triangles as shown in the assembly diagram.

2. Sew the blocks and side setting triangles together into diagonal rows. Press the seams in opposite directions from row to row. Sew the rows together; press. Finish by adding the corner setting triangles; press.

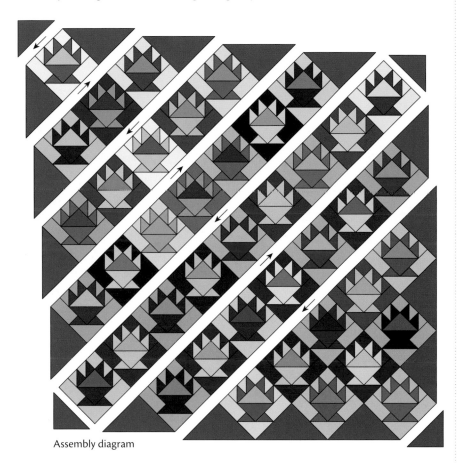

Assembly diagram

ADDING THE BORDERS

1. Sew the 2"-wide striped strips together end to end. From this strip, cut 4 inner-border strips 2" × 44½".

2. Refer to Partial-Seam Borders (page 74). Beginning with the right-hand edge and working counterclockwise, sew a 2" × 44½" inner-border strip to the right-hand edge, the top edge, the left-hand edge, and the bottom edge of the quilt. Press the seams toward the border.

3. Sew the 7" × 46" large-scale floral outer-border strips to the sides of the quilt. Press the seams toward the outer border. Sew the 7" × 59" outer-border strips to the top and bottom; press.

FINISHING

Refer to Finishing Your Quilt (page 77).

1. Layer and baste the quilt, and then quilt as desired. Diana machine quilted a crosshatched grid over the center of the quilt, a continuous swirl in the inner border, and a fanciful feather motif in the outer border.

2. Sew the 2⅛"-wide dark purple print strips together end to end with diagonal seams, and use them to bind the edges.

Birds
IN THE AIR

Designed and pieced by Alex Anderson. Machine quilted by Paula Reid.

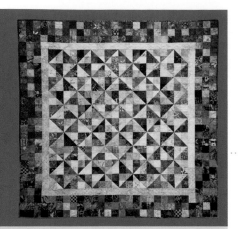

Finished quilt size: 56½" × 56½"

Finished block size: 4" × 4"

Total number of Birds in the Air blocks: 100

Skill level: *Confident beginner*

MATERIALS

Fabric amounts are based on a 42" fabric width.

Assorted light prints: 1¼ yards total for blocks

Assorted medium to dark prints: 1¼ yards total for blocks

Assorted blue, green, blue-green, and purple prints: ⅞ yard total for pieced border

Assorted red, pink, orange, and yellow prints: ⅞ yard total for pieced border

Assorted light tone-on-tone prints: ½ yard total for inner border

Assorted cool and warm prints: ½ yard total for binding

Backing: 3½ yards of fabric

Batting: 61" × 61" piece

I had fun digging into my stash of batiks to make this quilt. Birds in the Air is one of those wonderful blocks that divides in half on the diagonal, which gives the block, and the resulting quilt, lots of potential for movement and for creating secondary designs. I decided to focus on two color families for the pieced borders, but notice that I didn't divide them evenly.

CUTTING

All measurements include ¼"-wide seam allowance. Cut strips on the crosswise grain of the fabric (selvage to selvage). See the introduction to Piecing the Blocks (page 43) for the number and combination of pieces you'll use for each block.

From the assorted light prints

◻ Cut 100 squares 2⅞" × 2⅞" for blocks; cut each square in half once diagonally to make 200 half-square triangles.

◻ Cut 100 squares 2½" × 2½" for blocks.

From the assorted dark prints

◻ Cut 100 squares 2⅞" × 2⅞" for blocks; cut each square in half once diagonally to make 200 half-square triangles.

◻ Cut 100 squares 2½" × 2½" for blocks.

From the assorted cool prints (blues, greens, blue-greens, purples)

◻ Cut 150 squares 2½" × 2½" for the pieced border.

From the assorted warm prints (reds, pinks, oranges, yellows)

◻ Cut 150 squares 2½" × 2½" for the pieced border.

From the assorted light tone-on-tone prints

◻ Cut strips 2½" wide to total approximately 200".

From the assorted cool and warm prints

◻ Cut strips 2⅛" wide to total 240".

PIECING THE BLOCKS

These blocks are *completely* scrappy! For each block, use 2 half-square triangles 2⅞″ and a square 2½″ × 2½″, all cut from different light prints; and 2 half-square triangles 2⅞″ and a square 2½″ × 2½″, all cut from different dark prints.

1. Sew 2 scrappy light triangles 2⅞″ to adjacent sides of a light 2½″ × 2½″ square; press.

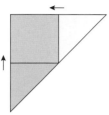

Sew triangles to square.

2. Sew 2 scrappy dark triangles 2⅞″ to adjacent sides of a dark 2½″ × 2½″ square; press.

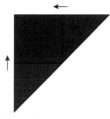

Sew triangles to square.

3. Sew the units from Steps 1 and 2 together along their long edges; press.

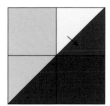

Sew units together.

4. Repeat Steps 1–3 to make a total of 100 scrappy blocks.

QUILT ASSEMBLY

1. Arrange the blocks in 10 horizontal rows of 10 blocks each, turning the blocks as shown in the assembly diagram.

2. Sew the blocks together into rows. Press seams in alternating directions from row to row. Sew the rows together; press.

Assembly diagram

ADDING THE BORDERS

1. Sew the 2½"-wide light tone-on-tone print strips together end to end. From this strip, cut 2 inner-border strips 2½" × 40½" and 2 inner-border strips 2½" × 44½".

2. Sew the 2½" × 40½" inner-border strips to the sides of the quilt. Press the seams toward the inner border. Sew the 2½" × 44½" inner-border strips to the top and bottom of the quilt; press.

3. Sew 3 cool-color 2½" squares together as shown; press. Make 48 units.

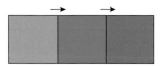

Make 48.

4. Sew 3 warm-color 2½" squares together; press. Make 48 units.

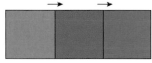

Make 48.

5. Sew the remaining cool and warm 2½" squares together into units of 3, mixing the cool and warm colors in each unit as shown; press. Make a total of 4 mixed units.

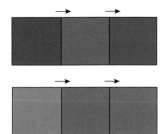

Make 2 of each.

6. Sew 22 units from Step 3 together; press. Sew this pieced border to the bottom of the quilt; press.

Sew units together.

7. Sew 22 units from Step 4 together; press. Sew this pieced border to the top of the quilt. Press the seams toward the inner border.

Sew units together.

8. Refer to the quilt photo (page 41). Sew 28 of the remaining units from Steps 3 and 4 together, using the units from Step 5 to transition from the cool to the warm colors; press. Make 2.

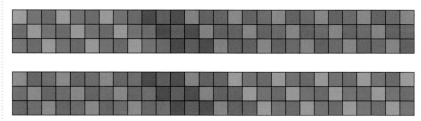

Sew remaining units together.

9. Refer to the quilt photo and sew the pieced borders from Step 8 to the sides of the quilt; press.

FINISHING

Refer to Finishing Your Quilt (page 77).

1. Layer and baste the quilt, and then quilt as desired. Paula machine quilted a design with lots of soft, fanciful curves in the center of the quilt and accented it with diagonal lines out to the inner border. She added a rickrack-like design in the inner border and a feathered vine in the outer border.

2. Sew the assorted 2⅛"-wide cool and warm print strips together end to end with diagonal seams, and use them to bind the edges.

Seeing Stars

Designed and pieced by Alex Anderson. Machine quilted by Dianne Schweickert.

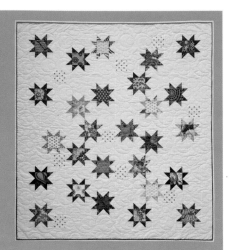

I love Star quilts, so I guess it's no surprise that I would include one in this book. I decided to emphasize the star motif by making the star points darker than the star centers (or "bellies") and— taking my cue from modern quilters—chose a fresh, sparkling white for the background. As a finishing touch, I dropped in a few random polka dot squares for visual interest and to complement the polka dots I used in some of the blocks.

Finished quilt size: 48½" × 54½"

Finished block size: 6" × 6"

Total number of Star blocks: 27

Skill level: *Confident beginner*

MATERIALS

Fabric amounts are based on a 42" fabric width.

Assorted light to dark colorful prints: 1 yard total for stars

White solid: 3 yards for block backgrounds, filler strips, filler squares, outer border, and binding

Light print: ¼ yard for filler squares

A teal and a blue subtle print: ⅛ yard of each for flat piping

Backing: 3 yards of fabric (horizontal seam)

Batting: 53" × 59" piece

CUTTING

All measurements include ¼"-wide seam allowance. Cut strips on the crosswise grain of the fabric (selvage to selvage) unless otherwise noted. See the introduction to Piecing the Blocks (page 47) for the number and combination of pieces you'll use for each block.

From the assorted colorful prints

☐ Cut 108 squares 2⅜" × 2⅜" in matching sets of 4 for star points.

☐ Cut 27 squares 3½" × 3½" for star centers.

From the *lengthwise grain* of the white solid

☐ Cut 2 strips 3½" × 42½".

☐ Cut 2 strips 3½" × 54½".

From the remaining white solid

☐ Cut 27 squares 4¼" × 4¼" for star-point units.

☐ Cut 108 squares 2" × 2" for block corners.

☐ Cut 11 squares 6½" × 6½" for large filler squares.

☐ Cut 20 rectangles 3½" × 6½" for filler strips.

☐ Cut 4 rectangles 3½" × 12½" for filler strips.

☐ Cut 1 rectangle 3½" × 9½" for filler strip.

☐ Cut 4 squares 3½" × 3½" for small filler squares.

☐ Cut 6 strips 2⅛" × the fabric width for binding.

From the light print

☐ Cut 9 squares 3½" × 3½" for filler squares.

From each of the blue and the teal prints

☐ Cut 3 strips 1" × the fabric width.

PIECING
THE BLOCKS

For each of these blocks, use 4 matching 2⅜″ × 2⅜″ squares for the star points, a square 3½″ × 3½″ cut from a different print for the star center, and a square 4¼″ × 4¼″ and 4 squares 2″ × 2″ cut from the white solid for the background.

1. Refer to Secret Star Method (page 73). Use 4 matching print squares 2⅜″ × 2⅜″ and a white square 4¼″ × 4¼″ to make 4 flying-geese units.

Make 4 flying-geese units.

2. Arrange the 4 units from Step 1, an assorted print 3½″ × 3½″ square, and 4 white 2″ × 2″ squares as shown. Sew the units and squares together into rows; press. Sew the rows together; press.

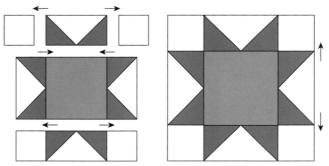

Sew units and squares together into rows.

3. Repeat Steps 1 and 2 to make a total of 27 Star blocks.

QUILT ASSEMBLY

1. Arrange the blocks, the large and small filler squares, and the filler strips as shown in the assembly diagram.

2. Sew the blocks, squares, and strips together in "neighborhoods" as shown; press.

3. Sew the neighborhoods together; press so that seams fall in opposite directions whenever possible.

4. Sew the 3½″ × 42½″ white outer-border strips to the top and bottom of the quilt. Press the seams toward the border. Sew the 3½″ × 54½″ white outer-border strips to the sides of the quilt; press.

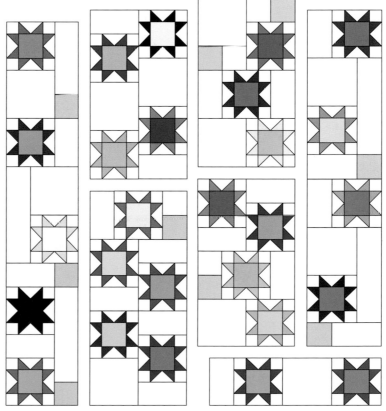

Assembly diagram

FINISHING

Refer to Finishing Your Quilt (page 77).

1. Layer and baste the quilt, and then quilt as desired. Dianne machine quilted an overall motif of large bubbles and swirls over the entire quilt, picking up on the circles in the many polka dot fabrics.

2. Sew the 1″-wide blue and teal strips together end to end with diagonal seams, and press the seams open. Fold the strip in half, wrong sides together, and press.

3. Trim the batting and backing even with the raw edges of the quilt top. Measure the quilt through the center from top to bottom and from side to side. Cut 2 strips to each measurement from the folded blue/teal strip. With right sides together and raw edges aligned, use a machine basting stitch and a scant ¼″ seam to sew the piping strips to the sides, top, and bottom of the quilt.

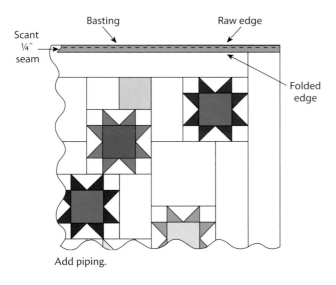

Add piping.

4. Sew the 2⅛″-wide white binding strips together end to end with diagonal seams, and use them to bind the edges of the quilt.

Double FLYING GEESE

Designed and pieced by Alex Anderson. Machine quilted by Dianne Schweickert.

When I started this book, I hadn't really thought about making a scrap quilt entirely from solids, but then I thought, "Why not?" Solids are scraps, too. You still have color and value to work with for contrast; the only missing ingredient is character of print, and with a wide variety of the two first elements, it's pretty easy to work around that. The key to this quilt was in mixing up those black backgrounds. Some are inky black, some more deep charcoal, some even a touch lighter. As for the geese, don't be afraid to toss in a few of those lighter hues. They may seem out of place among the jewel tones at first, but once you've made a couple and spread them around, they'll fit in just fine!

Finished quilt size: 49½″ × 57½″

Finished block size: 4″ × 4″

Total number of Double Flying Geese blocks: 80

Skill level: *Confident beginner*

MATERIALS

Fabric amounts are based on a 42″ fabric width.

Assorted black and dark gray solids: 2⅝ yards total for block backgrounds and outer border

Assorted colorful solids: 1⅜ yards total for geese and outer-border inserts

Black solid: ¾ yard for inner border and binding*

Backing: 3⅛ yards of fabric

Batting: 54″ × 62″ piece

* This can be the same as a black solid that you use for the block backgrounds.

CUTTING

All measurements include ¼″-wide seam allowance. Cut strips on the crosswise grain of the fabric (selvage to selvage). See the introduction to Piecing the Blocks (page 51) for the number and combination of pieces you'll use for each block.

From the assorted black and dark gray solids

- Cut 160 squares 2⅞″ × 2⅞″ for blocks.

- Cut 6 strips 8″ × the fabric width for outer borders.

From the assorted colorful solids

- Cut 40 squares 5¼″ × 5¼″ for geese.

- Cut 60 strips ¾″ × 8″ for border inserts.

- Cut 60 squares ¾″ × ¾″ for border inserts.

From the black solid

- Cut 4 strips 2½″ × the fabric width.

- Cut 6 strips 2⅛″ × the fabric width.

PIECING THE BLOCKS

A 5¼" colorful solid square and 4 black or gray solid 2⅞" squares will yield 4 flying-geese units.

1. Refer to Secret Star Method (page 73). Use 4 assorted black or dark gray solid squares 2⅞" × 2⅞" and a colorful square 5¼" × 5¼" to make 4 flying-geese units.

Make 4 flying-geese units.

2. Repeat Step 1 to make a total of 160 flying-geese units.

3. Sew the units from Step 2 together in pairs; press. Make 80 blocks.

Make 80 blocks.

QUILT ASSEMBLY

1. Arrange the blocks in 10 horizontal rows of 8 blocks each, turning the blocks as shown in the assembly diagram.

2. Sew the blocks together into rows. Press the seams in alternating directions from row to row. Sew the rows together; press.

Assembly diagram

MAKING AND ADDING THE BORDERS

The pieced outer borders of this quilt add lots of personality. The method for creating them is somewhat random and free-form, so have fun with the process. Refer to Borders with Mitered Corners (page 75) for guidance as needed with the final step.

1. Trim 2 black inner-border strips to measure 2½" × 40½". Trim the remaining inner-border strips to measure 2½" × 36½".

2. Sew the 2½" × 40½" black inner-border strips to the sides of the quilt. Press the seams toward the border. Sew the 2½" × 36½" black inner-border strips to the top and bottom of the quilt; press.

3. Cut each ¾"-wide colored strip into 2 segments. Sew a contrasting ¾" square between the 2 strips; press. Make 60 units now, cutting each strip into 2 pieces randomly for variety. (You can cut and make additional units later if you need them.) Refer to the quilt photo (page 49) for guidance as needed.

Make 60.

4. From 2 different 8"-wide black or gray strips, cut a segment approximately 4"–6" long. With right sides facing up, overlap the ends of the segments 1"–2" and cut the overlapped edges in a very gentle curve.

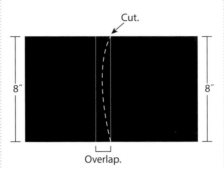

Overlap ends and cut curve.

5. Sew a pieced insert from Step 3 between the curved edges of the 2 black/gray segments you cut in Step 4; press.

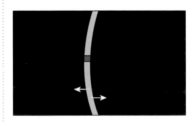

Sew pieced insert between curved edges.

6. Cut a few more segments from the 8"-wide black or gray strips, varying the length of the segments as desired. Using a new segment, and working from an end of the unit you stitched in Step 5, overlap, cut, and insert a new strip; press. Repeat the process, building the border as you go. You will need a total of 4 border units: 2 measuring approximately 54" long for the top and bottom borders, and 2 measuring approximately 62" long for the side borders.

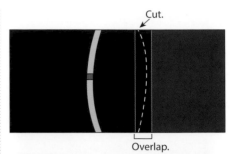

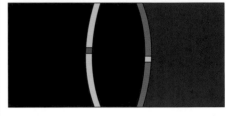

Overlap, cut, and insert new strips.

7. Trim each completed border unit to measure 7" wide.

8. Sew the 62"-long border units to the sides of the quilt and the 54"-long borders to the top and bottom, mitering the corners.

FINISHING

Refer to Finishing Your Quilt (page 77).

1. Layer and baste the quilt, and then quilt as desired. Dianne machine quilted a crosshatched grid over the center of the quilt and undulating lines in the outer, pieced border.

2. Sew the 2⅛"-wide black binding strips together end to end with diagonal seams and use them to bind the edges of the quilt.

Shoo Fly VARIATION

Designed and pieced by Carolyn Hughey. Machine quilted by Dianne Schweickert.

Finished quilt size: 55½" × 65½"

Finished block size: 10" × 10"

Total number of Shoo Fly blocks: 20

Skill level: *Confident beginner*

MATERIALS

Fabric amounts are based on a 42" fabric width.

Assorted 30s-style light-medium to medium-dark prints: 2 yards total for blocks and pieced Border 4

White solid: 3 yards for block backgrounds, Border 3, pieced Border 4, and binding

Light pink tone-on-tone print: ⅜ yard for Border 1*

Medium green tone-on-tone print: ½ yard for Border 2*

Backing: 3½ yards of fabric (horizontal seam)

Batting: 60" × 70" piece

* This can be the same fabric as an assorted print that you use for the blocks and pieced Border 4.

For a long time, I wasn't intuitively drawn to 1930s reproduction fabrics, but—ever one for a challenge—I decided I needed to give them a try. I purchased a few bundles of 30s prints, used them for a quilt or two, and guess what? I discovered that I liked working with them! Moral of the story: Don't be afraid to jump in and try something that doesn't come naturally. You may surprise yourself.

CUTTING

All measurements include ¼"-wide seam allowance. Cutting is given for a single block. Cut as you go, or cut the total number given in parentheses. Cut strips on the crosswise grain of the fabric (selvage to selvage), unless otherwise noted. See the introduction to Piecing the Blocks (page 55) for the number and combination of pieces you'll use for each block.

SHOO FLY BLOCK (20 TOTAL)

From a 30s-style print

■ Cut 4 squares 2⅞" × 2⅞" (80 total); cut each square in half once diagonally to make 8 half-square triangles.

■ Cut 4 squares 2½" × 2½" (80 total).

From a second 30s-style print

■ Cut 4 squares 2⅞" × 2⅞" (80 total); cut each square in half once diagonally to make 8 half-square triangles.

BORDERS AND BINDING

From the assorted 30s-style prints

■ Cut 12 squares 6¼" × 6¼" for pieced Border 4; cut each square in half twice diagonally to make 48 quarter-square triangles.

From the white solid

■ Cut 2 strips on the *lengthwise grain* 2½" × 56½".

■ Cut 2 strips on the *lengthwise grain* 2½" × 50½".

From the remaining white solid

■ Cut 160 squares 2⅞" × 2⅞" for block backgrounds; cut each square in half once diagonally to make 320 half-square triangles.

■ Cut 100 squares 2½" × 2½" for block backgrounds.

■ Cut 11 squares 6¼" × 6¼" for pieced Border 4; cut each square in half twice diagonally to make 44 quarter-square triangles.

■ Cut 7 strips 2⅛" × the fabric width.

From the pink tone-on-tone print

■ Cut 5 strips 2" × the fabric width.

From the green tone-on-tone print

■ Cut 6 strips 2" × the fabric width.

PIECING THE BLOCKS

For each of these blocks, you'll use 8 half-square triangles 2⅞" and 4 squares 2½" × 2½" cut from a 30s-style print; 8 half-square triangles 2⅞" cut from a second 30s-style print; and 16 half-square triangles 2⅞" and 5 squares 2½" × 2½" cut from the white solid.

1. Sew a print half-square triangle 2⅞" and a white half-square triangle 2⅞" together along their long edges; press. Make 8 matching units. Repeat with the second print.

Sew triangles together. Make 8 of each.

2. Arrange the half-square triangle units from Step 1, the 4 matching 2½" squares, and 5 white 2½" squares in 5 rows as shown. Sew the units and squares together into rows; press. Sew the rows together; press.

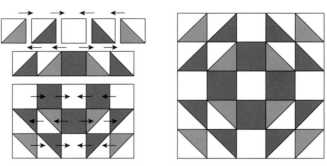

Sew units and squares into rows and sew rows together.

3. Repeat Steps 1 and 2 to make a total of 20 blocks.

QUILT ASSEMBLY

1. Arrange the blocks in 5 horizontal rows of 4 blocks each as shown in the assembly diagram.

2. Sew the blocks together into rows. Press the seams in alternating directions from row to row. Sew the rows together; press.

Assembly diagram

MAKING AND ADDING THE BORDERS

1. Sew the 2″-wide pink print strips together end to end. From this strip, cut 2 Border 1 strips 2″ × 50½″ and 2 Border 1 strips 2″ × 43½″.

2. Sew the 2″ × 50½″ Border 1 strips to the sides of the quilt. Press the seams toward the border. Sew the 2″ × 43½″ Border 1 strips to the top and bottom of the quilt; press.

3. Sew the 2″-wide green print strips together end to end. From this strip, cut 2 Border 2 strips 2″ × 53½″ and 2 Border 2 strips 2″ × 46½″.

4. Sew the 2″ × 53½″ Border 2 strips to the sides of the quilt. Press the seams toward the newly added border. Sew the 2″ × 46½″ Border 2 strips to the top and bottom of the quilt; press.

5. Sew the 2½″ × 56½″ white solid Border 3 strips to the sides of the quilt. Press the seams toward Border 2. Sew the 2½″ × 50½″ white solid Border 3 strips to the top and bottom of the quilt; press.

6. Arrange 13 quarter-square print triangles 6¼″ and 12 quarter-square white triangles 6¼″, alternating them. Sew the triangles together; press the seams toward the print triangles. Make 2 Border 4 units for the sides of the quilt.

Make 2.

7. Arrange 11 quarter-square print triangles 6¼″ and 10 quarter-square white triangles 6¼″, alternating them. Sew the triangles together; press the seams toward the print triangles. Make 2 Border 4 units for the top and bottom.

Make 2.

8. Sew the border units from Step 6 to the sides of the quilt. Press the seams toward the newly added border. Sew the border units from Step 7 to the top and bottom of the quilt, mitering the corners; press. Refer to Borders with Mitered Corners (page 75) for guidance when sewing the diagonal seam if needed.

Sew border units to quilt top.

FINISHING

Refer to Finishing Your Quilt (page 77).

1. Layer and baste the quilt, and then quilt as desired. Dianne machine quilted a crosshatched grid over the center of the quilt, a small whimsical swirl in the pink border, and a casual feathered garland over the remaining 3 borders.

2. Sew the 2⅛″-wide white strips together end to end with diagonal seams, and use them to bind the edges.

Scrappy SAMPLER

Designed and pieced by Alex Anderson. Machine quilted by Dianne Schweickert.

Sampler quilts make great scrap quilts, and they are especially fun when you toss a variety of blocks into the mix. The key is to work with blocks that are mathematically compatible—for example, evenly divisible by two or three—although you can compensate with plain filler strips, or strips of squares or half-square triangles, if you need to even things out. It was fun to make this quilt entirely from nineteenth-century repro fabrics, even those oddball oranges and acid greens. They're the ones that make this quilt sing!

Finished quilt size: 52½" × 56½"

Number of blocks / finished sizes:

- **9 Star blocks:** 6" × 6"
- **16 Basket blocks:** 6" × 6"
- **5 Shoo Fly blocks:** 6" × 6"
- **21 Bow Tie blocks:** 4" × 4"
- **46 Birds in the Air blocks:** 4" × 4"
- **4 Four-Patch blocks:** 4" × 4"
- **74 Flying Geese blocks:** 2" × 4"

Skill level: *Confident beginner*

MATERIALS

Fabric amounts are based on a 42" fabric width.

Assorted light to dark prints: 6¼ yards total for blocks

Multicolored stripe: ¼ yard for side inner border

Rust stripe: ½ yard for binding

Backing: 3¼ yards of fabric (horizontal seam)

Batting: 57" × 61" piece

CUTTING

All measurements include ¼"-wide seam allowance. Cut strips on the crosswise grain of the fabric (selvage to selvage). The cutting is given for a single block unless otherwise noted; totals are shown in parentheses.

STAR BLOCK (9 TOTAL)

From 1 print for background
- Cut 1 square 4¼" × 4¼" (9).
- Cut 4 squares 2" × 2" (36).

From a contrasting print for star points
- Cut 4 squares 2⅜" × 2⅜" (36).

From a third print for block center
- Cut 1 square 3½" × 3½" (9).

BASKET BLOCK (16 TOTAL)

From 1 print for basket
- Cut 3 squares 2⅜" × 2⅜" (48 total); cut each square in half once diagonally to make 6 half-square triangles.
- Cut 1 square 3⅞" × 3⅞" (16 total); cut the square in half once diagonally to make 2 half-square triangles (1 is extra).

From a contrasting print for background
- Cut 2 squares 2⅜" × 2⅜" (32 total); cut each square in half once diagonally to make 4 half-square triangles.
- Cut 1 square 2" × 2" (16).
- Cut 2 rectangles 2" × 3½" (32).
- Cut 1 square 3⅞" × 3⅞" (16 total); cut the square in half once diagonally to make 2 half-square triangles (1 is extra).

From a third print for basket filling
- Cut 1 square 3⅞" × 3⅞" (16 total); cut the square in half once diagonally to make 2 half-square triangles (1 is extra).

SHOO FLY BLOCK (5 TOTAL)

From 1 print for background
- Cut 2 squares 2⅞" × 2⅞" (10 total); cut each square in half once diagonally to make 4 half-square triangles.
- Cut 4 squares 2½" × 2½" (20).

From a contrasting print for block corners
- Cut 2 squares 2⅞" × 2⅞" (10 total); cut each square in half once diagonally to make 4 half-square triangles.

From a third print for block center
- Cut 1 square 2½" × 2½" (5).

BOW TIE BLOCK (21 TOTAL)

From 1 print for bow tie

- ☐ Cut 2 squares 2½″ × 2½″ (42).
- ☐ Cut 2 squares 1½″ × 1½″ (42).

From a contrasting print for background

- ☐ Cut 2 squares 2½″ × 2½″ (42).

46 BIRDS IN THE AIR BLOCKS

From assorted light prints

- ☐ Cut 46 squares 2½″ × 2½″.
- ☐ Cut 46 squares 2⅞″ × 2⅞″; cut each square in half once diagonally to make 92 half-square triangles.

From assorted dark prints

- ☐ Cut 46 dark squares 2½″ × 2½″.
- ☐ Cut 46 dark squares 2⅞″ × 2⅞″; cut each square in half once diagonally to make 92 half-square triangles.

4 FOUR-PATCH BLOCKS

From assorted prints

- ☐ Cut 16 squares 2½″ × 2½″.

FLYING GEESE BLOCKS (74 TOTAL*)

From 1 print for geese

- ☐ Cut 1 square 5¼″ × 5¼″ (19).

From a contrasting print for background

- ☐ Cut 4 squares 2⅞″ × 2⅞″ (76).

2 HALF-SQUARE TRIANGLES (FILLER STRIP)

From assorted light prints

- ☐ Cut 2 squares 2⅞″ × 2⅞″; cut each square in half once diagonally to make 4 triangles (2 are extra).

From assorted dark prints

- ☐ Cut 2 squares 2⅞″ × 2⅞″; cut each square in half once diagonally to make 4 triangles (2 are extra).

INNER BORDER AND BINDING

From the multicolored stripe

- ☐ Cut 3 strips 1½″ × the fabric width.

From the rust stripe

- ☐ Cut 6 strips 2⅛″ × the fabric width.

Note that the Flying Geese blocks are made in matching sets of 4 using the Secret Star method (page 73). You will have 2 extra blocks.

PIECING THE STAR BLOCKS

Refer to *Seeing Stars*, Piecing the Blocks (page 47), and make a total of 9 scrappy Star blocks.

Make 9.

PIECING THE BASKET BLOCKS

Refer to *Baskets*, Block 1 (page 38) and Block 2 (page 39), and make a total of 16 scrappy Basket blocks.

Make 16.

PIECING THE SHOO FLY BLOCKS

1. Sew a 2⅞″ half-square triangle and a contrasting 2⅞″ half-square triangle together along their long edges. Press the seam toward the darker triangle. Make 4 matching units.

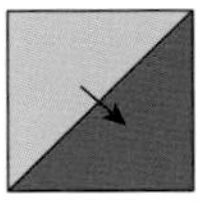

Make 4.

2. Arrange the 4 units from Step 1 with 4 matching 2½″ background squares and a contrasting 2½″ square. Sew the units and squares together into rows; press. Sew the rows together; press.

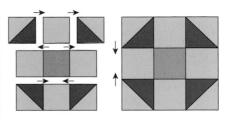

Sew units and squares into rows and sew rows together.

3. Repeat Steps 1 and 2 to make a total of 5 Shoo Fly blocks.

PIECING THE BOW TIE BLOCKS

Refer to *Bow Ties*, Block 1 and Block 2 (page 34), and make a total of 21 scrappy Bow Tie blocks.

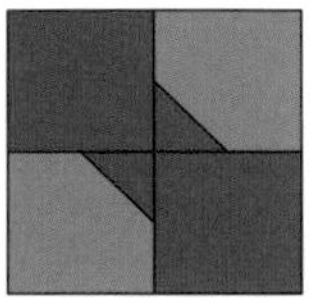

Make 21.

PIECING THE BIRDS IN THE AIR BLOCKS

Refer to *Birds in the Air*, Piecing the Blocks (page 43), and make a total of 46 scrappy Birds in the Air blocks.

Make 46.

PIECING THE FOUR-PATCH BLOCKS

Arrange 4 scrappy squares 2½" × 2½" in 2 rows. Sew the squares into rows; press. Sew the rows together; press. Make 4.

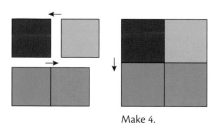

Make 4.

PIECING THE FLYING GEESE BLOCKS

Refer to Secret Star Method (page 73) and make a total of 76 Flying Geese blocks. You will have 2 extra blocks.

Make 76.

PIECING THE HALF-SQUARE TRIANGLE FILLER STRIP

1. Sew 2 contrasting 2⅞" half-square triangles together along their long edges. Press the seam toward the darker triangle. Make 2.

Make 2.

2. Sew the units from Step 1 together; press.

Make 1.

QUILT ASSEMBLY

1. Arrange the Basket, Star, and Shoo Fly blocks, 17 of the Bow Tie blocks, and the half-square triangle filler strip as shown in the assembly diagram.

2. Sew the blocks and filler strip together in "neighborhoods" as shown in the assembly diagram; press so that seams fall in opposite directions whenever possible.

3. Sew the neighborhoods together; press.

4. Refer to the quilt photo (page 57) and the assembly diagram (page 61). Arrange 20 Flying Geese blocks in a row to make a side border. Sew the blocks together; press all in the same direction. Make 2.

5. Sew the units from Step 4 to the sides of the quilt. Press the seams toward the quilt center.

6. Referring to the assembly diagram, arrange 17 Flying Geese blocks in a row to make a top/bottom border. Sew the blocks together; press all in the same direction. Make 2.

7. Sew a Bow Tie block to each end of the units from Step 6; press. Make 2 border units and sew them to the top and bottom of the quilt; press.

Assembly diagram

Add border units to quilt top.

ADDING THE BORDERS

1. Sew the 1½"-wide striped strips together end to end. From this strip, cut 2 inner-border strips 1½" × 48½".

2. Sew the 1½"-wide strips from Step 1 to the sides of the quilt. Press the seams toward the border.

3. Arrange 12 Birds in the Air blocks in a row, changing direction as shown in the quilt assembly diagram above. Sew the blocks together; press. Make 2 border units.

4. Sew the border units from Step 3 to the sides of the quilt. Press the seams toward the inner border.

5. Arrange 11 Birds in the Air blocks in a row, changing direction as shown in the diagram with border units above. Sew the blocks together; press. Make 2.

6. Sew a Four-Patch block to both ends of each unit from Step 5; press. Make 2 border units and sew them to the top and bottom of the quilt; press.

FINISHING

Refer to Finishing Your Quilt (page 77).

1. Layer and baste the quilt, and then quilt as desired. Dianne machine quilted a consistently sized crosshatched grid over the entire quilt, broken only by a cable motif in the flying-geese borders.

2. Sew the 2⅛"-wide rust binding strips together end to end with diagonal seams, and use them to bind the edges.

Gallery

Red and Green Zigzag
55½″ × 70¼″
made by Jan Magee
Denver, Colorado

Jan has taken a few simple shapes and a traditional holiday palette—red and green—and given them her own unique twist, resulting in a fresh, vibrant, and original design.

Pineapple Spray
45" × 60"
made by Carolyn Hughey
Boise, Idaho

I love how Carolyn created a fabulous color-wash effect by manipulating the values of the fabrics in this quilt, placing the lightest fabrics in the upper corner and working her way to the darker fabrics at the bottom of the design.

Photo by Sharon Risedorph

Strippy Star
approximately 92″ × 92″
maker unknown

From the collection of Julie Silber and Jean Demeter, The Quilt Complex. We'll likely never know why this unknown nineteenth-century quiltmaker made the design choices that she did, but her liberal use of white and gray gives this quilt a very modern look.

Easter Baskets
50″ × 48″
made by
Gwen Marston, Beaver Island, Michigan,
and Freddy Moran, Orinda, California.

Gwen and Freddy collaborated on this playful and
scrappy Liberated Basket quilt for their first book
together, *Collaborative Quilting*, published by
Sterling Publishing Co., Inc., in 2006.

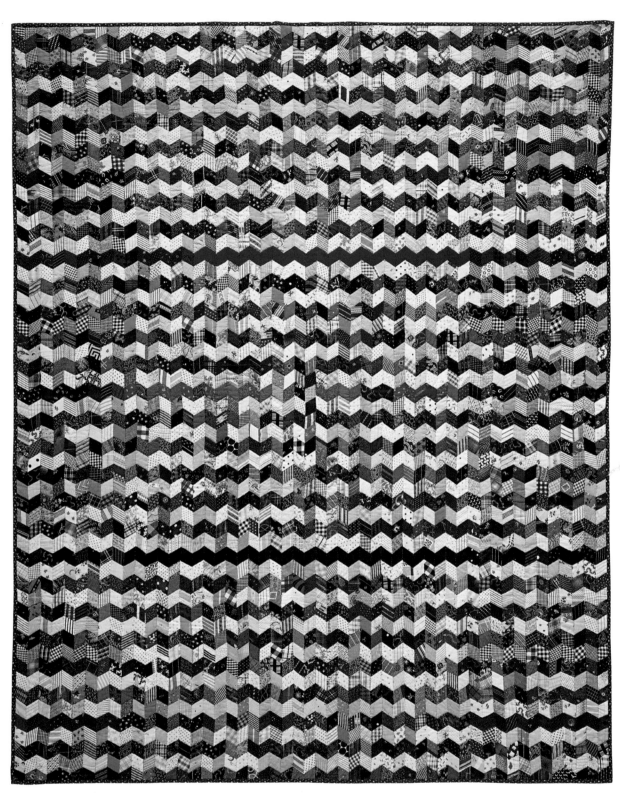

Vintage Zigzag
65″ × 83″, 1910
maker unknown

From the collection of Diana McClun. Diana purchased this hand-pieced, hand-quilted quilt at the International Quilt Festival in Houston. Despite the apparent randomness of the fabric placement, you'll notice a few places where order prevails!

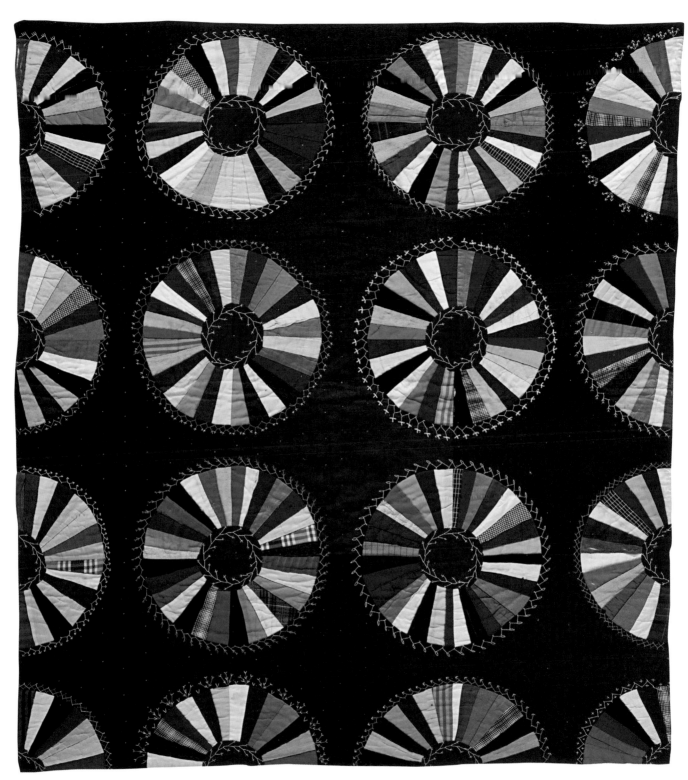

Wagon Wheels
70" × 79"
made by Louisa Zollinger Nuffer

From the collection of Diana McClun. This hand-tied wool quilt was made by Diana's grandmother some 30 years before Diana was born. Diana recalls scraps of wool being given away for free at the Utah Woolen Mills in Logan, Utah. She remembers going to the mill with her mother and grandmother and being lifted over the fence to bring back the "treasures."

Sensu (Fans)
58″ × 63″
made by
Diana McClun, Walnut Creek, California,
and Laura Nownes, Pleasant Hill, California.
Machine quilted by Valerie Simpson
of Creative Quilts.

Diana and Laura fell in love with the beautiful Japanese fabric by Hanamomen used in the sashing. The 9″ Fan blocks were strip pieced and then cut using a template for accurate curves, making this quilt easy enough for even a beginning quiltmaker. Pattern available (see Resources, page 79).

Bow Ties
64″ × 80″
made by
Diana McClun, Walnut Creek, California,
and Laura Nownes, Pleasant Hill, California.
Machine quilted by Kathy Sandbach.

In creating this quilt, Diana and Laura were aiming to design a Bow Tie quilt that was more about the overall light and dark design than the individual blocks. Compare their quilt with *Bow Ties* on page 32. Value placement does make a difference! Pattern available (see Resources, page 79). The quilt was made entirely of fabric designer Jennifer Sampou's first line of fabrics with P&B Textiles back in the early 90s.

Indigo Trips Around the World
85″ × 102″
made by Anabeth Dollins
Mt. Lebanon, Pennsylvania

Most of the blue and white fabrics surrounding the blocks came from batik workshops in Slovakia; others came from the Czech Republic, Indonesia, and Japan. Anabeth adapted the design from Bonnie Hunter's *Scrappy Trips Around the World*, using only fabrics from her stash. She says, "Unfortunately, the size of my stash didn't seem to diminish at all!"

Kaleidoscope
70″ × 70″
made by Kim McCloskey
Provo, Utah

Kim made this quilt using half-square triangles she collected while participating in the half-square triangle exchange initiated by Edyta Sitar's appearance on *The Quilt Show*. By the end of the exchange, some 250,000 half-square triangles had made their way around the globe. Kim's careful placement of lights and darks creates the fabulous overall pattern of this colorful quilt.

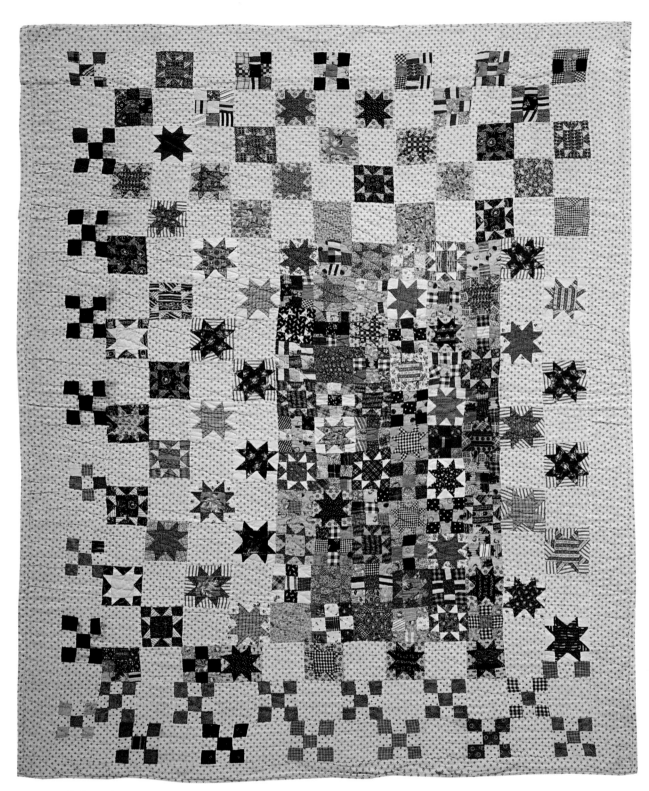

Universe
circa 1880, 58″ × 72″
maker unknown

From the collection of Julie Silber and Jean Demeter, The Quilt Complex.
This quilt combines two traditional patchwork patterns—Nine-Patch
and Variable Star; however, by organizing the light and dark fabrics in
a decidedly untraditional way, this nineteenth-century quiltmaker has
created a very personal and memorable quilt.

General Instructions

These instructions provide the basics that you need to construct a quilt.

Rotary Cutting

If you've never used a rotary cutter before, you might want to read *Rotary Cutting with Alex Anderson*. If the process is new to you, practice on some scrap fabric before starting on a project.

Pinning

Some quilters pin when they piece and some quilters don't. I'm a firm believer in pinning because I have found that the little time it takes to pin can determine the success of the block—and ultimately, the quilt. Basically, I pin wherever there are seams and intersections that need to line up.

I strongly recommend that you invest in a package or two of quality pins. My favorites are extra-fine (1⅜″ or 0.50mm) glass-head pins. They are a bit more expensive than regular pins, but believe me, they are worth the investment.

Piecing

Set the stitch length on your sewing machine just long enough so a seam ripper will slide nicely under the stitch. Backtacking is not necessary if the seam ends will be crossed by other seams. Use a ¼″ seam allowance unless otherwise instructed.

Pressing

I usually press seams to one side or the other, but in some cases—for example, if six or more seams are converging in one area—I press the seams open to reduce the bulk. I've included arrows on the illustrations to indicate which way to press the seams.

Secret Star Method

You'll love this easy and efficient method for making star-point units and flying-geese units four at a time. Measurements for the large and small squares are included in the specific project instructions.

1. Draw a diagonal line on the wrong side of each of the 4 smaller squares. This will be the cutting line. Draw a second set of lines ¼″ from the original diagonal line on both sides. These will be the sewing lines.

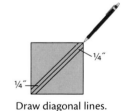

Draw diagonal lines.

2. Place 2 marked squares on opposite corners of the larger square as shown, right sides together. Stitch carefully on the 2 outer lines.

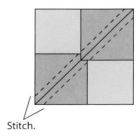

Stitch on outermost lines.

3. Cut on the line between the lines of stitching; press the units open.

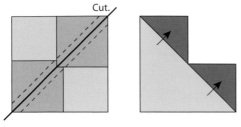

Cut on unsewn line and press.

4. Place a third marked square right sides together with the open corner of a unit from Step 3 as shown. Stitch on the 2 outer lines. Cut on the line between the lines of stitching. Repeat using the last marked square and the remaining unit from Step 3.

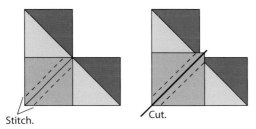

Stitch.   Cut.

Stitch and cut on unsewn line.

5. Press open. You now have 4 finished units!

Press.

Partial-Seam Borders

Sewing partial-seam borders onto a quilt is a lot like sewing the first row of strips around the center square of a Log Cabin block. Easy! I used the partial-seam-border technique to add the inner borders to *Baskets* (page 36). The cut measurements of the partial-seam borders are included in the *Baskets* instructions.

1. Find and mark the midpoint on each side of the quilt top.

2. Measure the *length* of the quilt top and mark this length on each side border. Find and crease the midpoint between the end of the strip and the point you've just marked. Repeat for the top and bottom borders, measuring and marking the *width* of the quilt top, and creasing to find the midpoint.

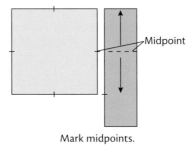

Mark midpoints.

3. Place a side border along the right-hand edge of the quilt top, right sides together. Match the midpoints and then match the bottom right-hand corner of the quilt top with the marked endpoint on the border, and pin. (The border will extend beyond the bottom edge of the quilt.) Align the opposite end of the border strip with the top right-hand corner of the quilt, and pin as needed.

4. Stitch the border strip to the quilt top, stopping approximately 3″ from the corner of the quilt top; press.

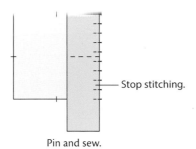

Stop stitching.

Pin and sew.

5. Place the top border along the top edge of the quilt top, right sides together. Match the midpoints and then match the ends of the border with the corners of the quilt. Pin as needed.

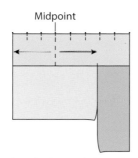

Midpoint

Match midpoints and pin top border.

6. Stitch the top border to the quilt; press.

7. Repeat to add the left side border and the bottom border.

8. Complete the first border seam. If necessary, trim and square the corners of the quilt.

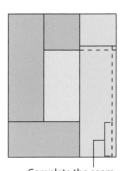
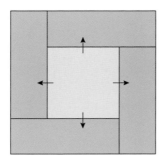

Complete the seam.

Complete seam and press.

Borders with Mitered Corners

Mitered borders have corner seams angled at 45° rather than 90°. These borders are a little trickier, but the results are well worth the effort. *Double Flying Geese* (page 49) is finished with a mitered outer border. The border lengths necessary for this quilt are given in the project instructions.

1. Find and mark the midpoint on each side of the quilt top and the midpoint of each border strip. From the marked midpoint, measure in both directions and mark half the *length* of the quilt top on each side border. Repeat using the *width* of the quilt top to measure and mark the top and bottom borders.

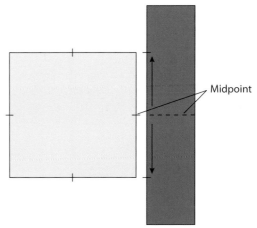

Midpoint

Measure and mark.

2. Place the side border and the quilt top right sides together. Match and pin the midpoints, and then match the corners of the quilt top with the marked ends of the border strip, and pin. The border will extend beyond the edges of the quilt top. Use additional pins as needed.

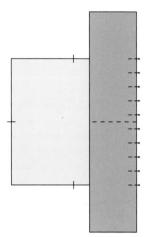

Match points and pin.

3. Stitch the border to the quilt top. Start and end the seam with a backstitch, ¼" in from the corners of the quilt top; press. Repeat for the other side, and the top and bottom borders.

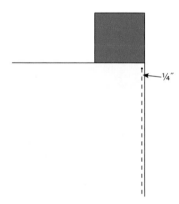

Start and end stitching ¼" from the corner. Backstitch at each end.

4. Lay a corner of the quilt right side up on an ironing board. Place a border strip on top of the neighboring border.

5. Fold the top border strip under, so it forms a 45° angle, and press lightly. Use a ruler with a 45° mark to check that the angle is accurate and that the corner of the quilt is flat and square. Make any necessary adjustments. When you're sure everything is in place, firmly press the fold.

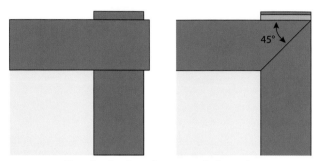

Place first border strip on top of other strip.
Fold border strip at 45° angle.

6. From the corner, fold the quilt top on the diagonal, right sides together, aligning the long raw edges of the neighboring border strips. The fold you've made in the border should form a perfect extension of the diagonal fold in the quilt top. Mark the fold line on the border with a pencil, and pin.

7. To sew the miter, backstitch at the inside corner, at the point where the borders meet, and then stitch along the marked fold toward the outside corner of the border. You'll be stitching on the bias, so be careful not to stretch the corner as you sew. Backstitch to finish. Trim the excess border fabric to a ¼" seam allowance, and press the seam open.

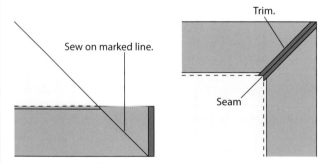

Fold quilt top to align fold lines. Sew and trim.

8. Repeat Steps 4–7 to miter the remaining corners.

Finishing Your Quilt

LAYERING AND BASTING

I typically cut my batting and backing 2″ larger than the quilt top on all sides. The amounts shown in the materials list for each project include this extra insurance.

Spread the backing wrong side up on a (nonloop) carpet or work surface. Smooth the backing, and secure it with T-pins or masking tape. Center the batting on top of the backing, and trim the two layers so the raw edges match. Center the quilt top right side up on the batting, smoothing carefully to remove any wrinkles.

For hand quilting, use large hand stitches to baste the three layers together in a 4″ grid pattern. For machine quilting, secure the three layers every 3″ with rustproof size 1 safety pins. Distribute the pins evenly, avoiding areas where you know you'll be stitching. For both hand and machine quilting, baste all the way to the edges of the quilt top.

The instructions for each project include a description of how the quilt was quilted. For additional suggestions regarding quilting a scrap quilt, see Thoughts on Quilting (page 29).

BINDING

1. Trim the batting and backing even with the raw edge of the quilt top.

2. Cut 2⅛″-wide strips from the fabric width as directed in the project instructions.

3. Sew the strips together end to end with a diagonal seam and press the seams open. Pressing this way will help prevent a big lump in the binding.

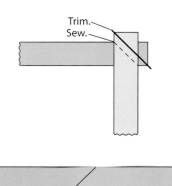

Join strips with diagonal seam.

4. Fold and press the binding in half lengthwise, wrong sides together.

5. With raw edges even, pin the binding to the edge of the quilt, starting a few inches from the corner and leaving the first few inches of the binding unattached. Start sewing, using a ¼″ seam allowance. For pucker-free bindings, use a walking foot or even-feed feature.

6. Stop ¼″ from the first corner, and backstitch a stitch.

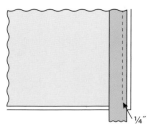

Stitch to ¼″ from corner.

7. Raise the needle and lift the presser foot. Rotate the quilt ¼ turn. Fold the binding at a right angle so it extends straight above the quilt and forms a 45° fold in the corner.

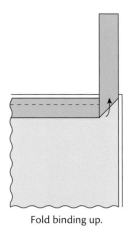

Fold binding up.

8. Bring the binding strip down even with the next edge of the quilt. Begin sewing at the folded edge. Stop ¼" from the next corner and backstitch a stitch.

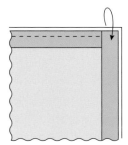

Fold binding down even with edge of quilt.

9. Repeat in the same manner at all corners. Stop sewing several inches from where you started stitching the binding to the quilt.

10. To trim the end of the binding, fold the ending binding tail back on itself where it meets the beginning of the binding. From the fold, measure and mark the cut width of the binding strip (2⅛"). Cut the ending binding tail to this measurement.

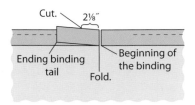

Trim binding.

11. Unfold both tails to create a single layer of fabric. Place a tail on top of the other at a right angle, right sides together. Mark a diagonal line and stitch on the line. Trim the seam allowance to ¼". Press the seam open. Refold the binding strip and finish stitching it to the quilt.

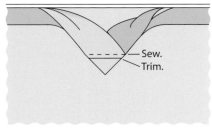

Join binding.

12. Turn the folded edge of the binding over the raw edge of the quilt and slipstitch the binding to the backing. Form miters at the corners.

QUILT LABEL

I always encourage quiltmakers to label their quilts. The information you include will be treasured for generations to come. Use a permanent fabric pen on the back (or even on the front) of the quilt or design a beautiful patch specifically for the quilt with embroidery or colorful fabric pens. Before sewing the label to the quilt, consider also writing directly on the quilt (where the label will cover) for assurance that the information will not be lost in case the label is removed.

Alex Anderson's love of quilting began in 1978 when she completed a Grandmother's Flower Garden quilt as part of the work toward her degree in art from San Francisco State University. Over the years, her central focus has been to understand fabric relationships; she has developed an intense appreciation of traditional quilts and beautiful quilting surface design.

Alex Anderson is the author of 30 books in 4 languages, selling nearly a million copies worldwide. Her quilts and instruction tips have also appeared in numerous magazines. She is the national spokesperson for Bernina of America, a promotional partner for AccuQuilt, a designer of her own line of fabrics with RJR Fabrics, and she has a line of threads with Superior Threads. For 11 years, she served as host of *Simply Quilts* on HGTV. Alex continues to be one of the most sought-after instructors and lecturers in the international quilting and sewing industry.

Alex is a founding partner, with Ricky Tims, of *The Quilt Show* (at thequiltshow.com) and *The QuiltLife* magazine (published by the American Quilter's Society). *The Quilt Show* is the world's first full-service interactive online video / web TV show created just for quilters worldwide. *The Quilt Show*'s mission is to educate, inspire, entertain, connect, and grow the world quilting community in a fun, positive, and interactive environment. *The QuiltLife* magazine celebrates the lifestyle of today's quiltmaker in a fresh and beautiful format.

Alex was chosen as the 2008 Silver Star Award winner given annually by the International Quilt Festival to a quilter "whose work and influence has made— and continues to make—a sizable and positive impact on the quilting industry and community."

Alex was also chosen by the readers of *Quilters Newsletter* magazine (February 2009) as "the most influential person in the quilting industry" (in a three-way tie with Ricky Tims and Karey Bresenhan of Quilts, Inc.).

Alex's personal mission is not only to share her love of quilting with anyone who will listen but to educate and encourage those interested in quilting as clearly and simply as possible, so quilting can continue to be handed down from generation to generation.

Alex lives in northern California with her husband.

www.alexandersonquilts.com
www.thequiltshow.com
www.thequiltlife.com

RESOURCES

Bernina (of America)
(630) 978-2500
www.bernina.com

C&T Publishing
Quick & Easy Block Tool
(925) 677-0377
www.ctpub.com

From Me to You Quilts
Patterns for *Sensu* (page 68)
and *Bow Ties* (page 69)

Laura Nownes on Etsy
www.etsy.com/shop/lnownes

Superior Threads
(800) 499-1777
www.superiorthreads.com

AccuQuilt
(888) 258-7913
www.accuquilt.com

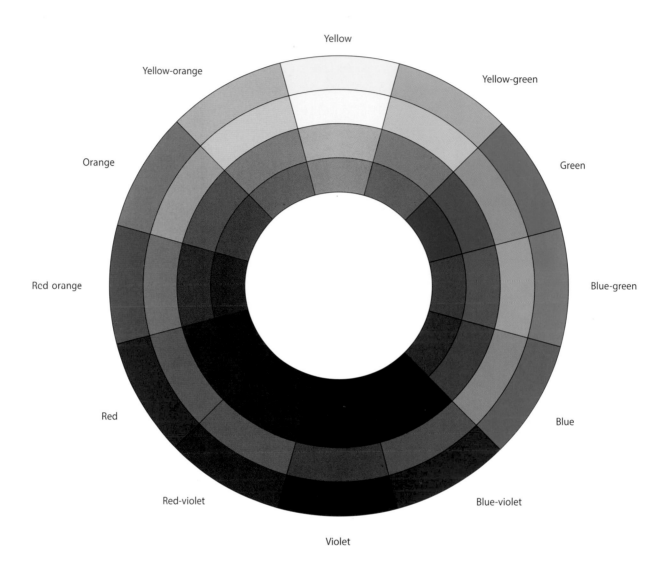

Yellow

Yellow-orange

Yellow-green

Orange

Green

Red orange

Blue-green

Red

Blue

Red-violet

Blue-violet

Violet

SCRAP QUILTING WITH ALEX ANDERSON